Praise for *Make*

"You've heard about the Science of Reading. This is a book about the science of history: How to plan the knowledge students need to have the richest and most informed discussions of major historical questions. For a student whose experience of history has been carefully shaped by teaching tools that do those things, the sky's the limit and this book is your roadmap."

—**Doug Lemov**, author of international bestseller *Teach Like a Champion*

"Worrell and Bambrick-Santoyo put all the pieces together in this excellent book. They provide models and examples of techniques that get young people thinking, talking, and doing history. From retrieval practice to high-level discourse, the book makes it all clear and accessible to teachers who want to take their game up a level."

—**Jonathan Bassett & Gary Shiffman**, authors of *From Story to Judgment: The Four Question Method for Teaching and Learning Social Studies*

"*Make History* brings an important and crucial perspective of historical context to light. It not only teaches the practical and essential way to learn, discuss, and understand history but also provides the significance of learning history through a variety of sources to affect student perspectives and, in turn, our future. As a History major and coach of teachers, *Make History* inspires me to get back into the classroom and utilize these replicable instructional strategies for bringing history to life!"

—**Amanda McDonald**, principal, Denver (Colorado) Public Schools

"*Make History* is a must-read for all leaders and educators who are eager to increase the rigor in History for all students. The book gives practical, easy-to-follow guidance on best practices that will affect how you teach History with a focus on equity and high expectations."

—**Laura Garza**, associate superintendent, Dallas (Texas) ISD

"When I was searching for what we were missing to help our students achieve, think, and learn, at a deeper level, the systems and tools of Paul Bambrick-Santoyo gave us a base, a true north for what good instruction looked like. Who better than he and Art Worrell to finally provide History teachers a resource to help facilitate deeper thinking and high expectations for our scholars.

This book is an exciting new tool in the arsenal of History educators around the world to maximize learning in their classrooms."

—**Dr. Jimmy D. Shaw Jr.**, superintendent, Florence (Alabama) City Schools

"Wherever I go, I bring my Paul Bambrick-Santoyo library with me! The ideas and materials in this book are practical and field-tested, and they provide all the required insight and resources needed to teach equity and high expectations without compromise."

—**Joshua Zoia**, country director, One World Network of Schools

"Paul Bambrick-Santoyo's research and subsequent teaching has lifted the quality of leader professional development in my school district. His ability to identify the levers that support improved student outcomes has changed the course of our work and the outcomes for our students."

—**Jacqueline Glasheen**, executive director of school leadership, Holyoke (Massachusetts) Public Schools

"*Make History* is an actionable guidebook for creating the rich, rigorous, and empowering History instruction that our young people deserve—and that our communities need."

—**Rachel Willcutts**, Director of Rhodes Scholarship, IDEA Public Schools

MAKE HISTORY

MAKE HISTORY

A Practical Guide for Middle and
High School History Instruction

Art Worrell
Paul Bambrick-Santoyo

JB JOSSEY-BASS™
A Wiley Brand

*"A generation which ignores history has
no past and no future."*
— Robert Heinlein

*"History is not a burden on the memory but an
illumination of the soul."*
— Lord Acton

*"People are trapped in history, and history is
trapped in them."*
— James Baldwin

Contents

Online Content

This book is supplemented with videos and print-ready materials. Visit this site for additional content: www.wiley.com/go/makehistory

APPENDIX—PRINT-READY MATERIALS

These online resources are ready for you to print and use in your classroom.

Resources	Description
Overview	• Arc of Teaching History • Make History Implementation Rubric
Part 1: Define the Destination	• Components of a Strong Prompt • Quick Resources for Finding Sources • Historical Thinking Skills (College Board) • AP Historical Reasoning Processes • Know-Show Chart Template • Planning Template—Intellectual Prep for Instruction
Part 2: Build Knowledge	• Build Knowledge Lesson Plan One-Pager • DEI Checklist • Sample Notebook Rubrics • Student Notetaking Examples • Check for Understanding: Four-Sentence Summary • Check for Understanding: Six-Panel Storyboard
Part 3: Grapple with Evidence	• Grapple with Evidence One-Pager • Four-Corner Annotation • Universal Prompts for Document Analysis • Monitoring Pathways: Rows and U-Shape

Resources	Description
Part 4: Make Sense of It Through Discourse	• Inquiry One-Pager • Habits of Discourse 101—Create Conversation • Habits of Discourse 201—Deepen Discourse • Universal Prompts for Discourse
Part 5: Stamp and Measure the Learning	• Characteristics of a Strong Task Assessment • Sample Task Assessment
Part 6: Sample Lesson Plans	AP US History: Reconstruction • Build Knowledge Lesson • Grapple with Evidence and Inquiry Lessons AP World History: Westernization or Southernization? • Build Knowledge Lesson • Grapple with Evidence and Inquiry Lessons 6th-grade History: Pre-Colombian North America • Build Knowledge Lesson • Grapple with Evidence & Inquiry lessons 8th-grade History: Westward Settlement • Build Knowledge Lesson • Grapple with Evidence & Inquiry lessons

VIDEOS
BUILD KNOWLEDGE (PART 2)

Clip	Technique	Description	Where Referenced in the Book
1	Class Oral Review	**"The Communists took over because the [Russian] people supported their slogan of 'bread and peace.'"** Dan Balmert's students review the major outcomes of WWI and WWII in preparation for discourse.	p. 65
2	Class Oral Review	**"What is the benefit of remembering events in chronological order when it comes to understanding history?"** Neha Marvania prompts students to connect chronology and causation to their analysis of Enlightenment-era revolutions.	p. 66

Clip	Technique	Description	Where Referenced in the Book
3	Opening Hook	**"So I want to draw a quick modern connection to what we're studying today."** Cat Lum draws a historical parallel between the economic concerns of 21st-century Midwestern voters and 19th-century Gilded Age farmers.	p. 75
4	Opening Hook	**"If you were an activist during this time, what do you think would be the most important issue to prioritize?"** Jillian Gaeta asks students to prioritize the issues facing African Americans following the Civil War by imagining themselves as Reconstruction-era activists.	p. 77

GRAPPLE WITH EVIDENCE (PART 3)

Clip	Technique	Description	Where Referenced in the Book
5	Build Skill— Guided Practice	**"Notice the key steps I take, strategies, or even questions that I ask myself while I go through this process."** Art Worrell models how to unpack an AP US history prompt in a guided practice think-aloud.	p. 101
6	Activate Skill/ Activate Knowledge	**"Annotate the prompt and identify the historical thinking skill. What do we already know about the debates and the antebellum period?"** After identifying the prompt's historical thinking skill, Michelle De Sousa's students activate prior knowledge of the Lincoln-Douglas debates.	p. 104
7	Monitoring— Circulate with Purpose	**"Is it a change or a continuity? Then tell me why and how it answers our prompt."** Brendan Kennedy reviews student writing as he monitors during independent work time.	p. 110

Clip	Technique	Description	Where Referenced in the Book
8	Monitoring—Name the Lap	**"I'm going to look at your point of view corner first."** Courtney Watkins names what she's looking for at the start of each lap.	p. 112

MAKE SENSE OF IT THROUGH DISCOURSE (PART 4)

Clip	Technique	Description	Where Referenced in the Book
9	Set the Stage for Discourse	**"Did these changes mark a social and/or constitutional revolution?"** Art Worrell's students debate whether Reconstruction should be considered a social and/or constitutional revolution.	p. 122
10	Rollout a Habit: Revoice	**"We are going to learn a new practice for discourse—revoicing. There are three ways you can authentically revoice something . . ."** Tom Brinkerhoff introduces and models a new discourse habit.	p. 128
11	Authentic Student Practice: Revoice	**"I see where you're coming from when you say that the theory of social death is useful, but Patterson's theory is actually a limitation."** Students in Tom Brinkerhoff's class revoice to debate a social theory used as framework to analyze global slavery.	p. 130
12	Deepen Discourse: Drop Knowledge	**"The Pinkerton Detectives [were] a private security force that businesses would hire to try to break up strikes."** Scott Kern gives students an essential piece of schema they'll need to analyze the causes of the 1892 Homestead Strike.	p. 144

Clip	Technique	Description	Where Referenced in the Book
13	Deepen Discourse: Sophisticate	**"Why weren't these challenges front and center to reformers?"** Art Worrell prompts students to add nuance to an overly simple argument about the outcomes of the Progressive Era.	p. 145
14	Deepen Discourse: Problematize	**"How is increased nationalism a social revolution, when we've seen high levels of nationalism throughout history?"** A student in Art Worrell's US History class respectfully challenges another student's assertion.	p. 146

STAMP AND MEASURE THE LEARNING (PART 5)

Clip	Technique	Description	Where Referenced in the Book
15	Stamp in Student Voice	**"The 1920s was and wasn't a time of liberation for women. Women got more opportunities . . . [but] society was still having them follow traditional values."** Students synthesize final thoughts after discourse.	p. 156

Acknowledgments

At its heart, teaching is a collective practice. And while the list of names we mention here is long, it is by no means exhaustive. Many have shaped our journey as educators. These acknowledgments shine a light on those who made *Make History* possible.

A special thank-you goes to social studies and history teachers featured in this book: Amir Ballard, Brendan Kennedy, Cat Lum, Courtney Watkins, Dan Balmert, Duncan Miller, Edward Acosta, Jah'Nique Campos, Jillian Gaeta, Michelle De Sousa, Neha Marvania, Rachel Blake, Scott Kern, and Tom Brinkerhoff. Your dedication to your students and love of history gave this book life. We especially want to thank the associate director of 5–8 History at Uncommon Schools, Rebecca Gomez. Your creativity, insight, and passion for history have been invaluable in the shaping of our work over the past five years.

We owe an incredible debt of gratitude to Doug Lemov, Colleen Driggs, Erica Woolway, and the whole Teach Like a Champion team. Your partnership and research helped us set such a clear vision for our work in knowledge retrieval back in 2018. It has been such a pleasure to collaborate with and learn from your phenomenal team of educators.

Many of the best practices featured in their classrooms were finetuned in working groups over the years. Thank you to those indefatigable members: Brian Pullen, Daly Murray, Kacey Paige, Jeffrey Miller, John Fox, Joshua Sullivan, Erica Lim, Maya Park, Sara Burns, Shauntia Harrison, Stephanie Irving, and Stephen Cassady. You combed through countless sets of data, video, lesson plans, and student work to name the moves that would take our students from good to great. To Julie Jackson and Brett Peiser, co-CEOs of our network of 55 schools and mentors to so many amazing educators throughout the country, thank you for your never-ending support and encouragement and for creating the space for the completion of this book. The support and feedback of the Uncommon Schools Curriculum and Assessment Team, led by Christine Algozo and Erin Michaels, was invaluable to the creation of *Make History*. Thank you to team members past and present for the resources, ideas, and friendship: Aisha Butcher, Allison Johnson, Amy Parsons, Danny Murray, Emelia Pelliccio, Julia Addeo, Kevin Ozoria, Lauren Schmidt, Sean Healey, and Steve Chiger. Your work allowed us to innovate and codify what we do in history and social studies instruction.

Our colleagues in academia and education shared our vision for powerful history instruction and the toolboxes to make it possible. Their work made ours better. Kudos to Abby Reisman, Brenda Santos, Eric Foner, Grant Wiggins, Jay McTighe, James Verrilli, Jon Bassett, Gary Shiffman, Sam Wineburg, Sonia Nieto, and Zaretta Hammond. We give special thanks to Joel Breakstone and the Stanford History Education Group. Their work has fundamentally shaped the way we teach history.

Many thanks to the Wiley team: Kezia Endsley, Amy Fandrei, Pete Gaughan, and Mary Beth Rosswurm. Thanks to those who gave feedback to those early drafts: Brett Peiser, Charles Mahoney, Dave Marshall, Jamielee Green, James Verrilli, Justin Rose, Kim Marshall, and Shana Pyatt. Your insights made the book what it is today. We are also grateful for our writing partner, Morayo Faleyimu, who nurtured the book from its earliest beginnings to its final form.

Art: The path that led me to this book was paved with the work and influence of so many people in my life. To Michael Mann, who saw something in me as a 21-year-old college kid and hired me as his founding middle school history teacher, thank you for being the best school principal I have ever known, for always believing in me, for being my advocate, and for never settling for anything less than the best for our students. You continue to inspire me. To Emily Mann and Jesse Rector: you were the two most important mentors whom I learned from in my first years of teaching. What I have learned from you continues to shape my work as an educator. To Mike Taubman, thank you for your brotherhood during this 18-year journey as educators. You have been there for me at my best and worst moments and your research and thought partnership helped to shape this book. To my mother, Joan Worrell, thank you for your quiet strength and undying love. The sacrifices that you and dad made for me gave me the chance to do what I love; there is no greater gift that I could have asked for. To my sister, Shana Pyatt, I am an educator because of you. Thank you for instilling a love of learning in me, for loving me unconditionally, and for being the best sister, mother, daughter, and aunt anyone could ask for. Thank you to my aunts Ana and Ina and my Uncle Fred. This book was written at a very challenging time in my life. Your love and support shepherded my mother, sister, and me through our darkest moments and allowed me the opportunity to complete this work. To Brian Worrell, the cousin who became my brother, thank you for always being willing to listen to ideas and share a laugh during the long hours of work on this text. To my amazing wife, Juliana, you've always challenged me to be my best self. I have learned so much from you as a transformative school leader and as the amazing mother of our three children. You are my muse. Without you, this book would not be possible. I love you and thank you for taking this journey through life with me. To my children, Arthur Jr., Gabriel, and Isabella. The joy that you three have brought to my life is immeasurable. This book has been a labor of love, and if I didn't have you three to escape to each day, I'm not sure that I could have done it. To Jay and Juliana Collins, thank you for your support and guidance and for being amazing grandparents to my children. To Jay Collins Jr., thank you for being a role model and uncle to my children and a brother to me. Last, thank you to my dad, Johnnie H. Worrell Sr., and my brother, Johnnie H. Worrell Jr. I miss you both beyond what words can describe. I write this book in honor of your memory.

Paul: I was only 17 years old when my high school teacher Donald Sprague pushed me to make connections between the past and the present, and I will never forget it. Such a seemingly small moment in class was a key turning point in the trajectory of my life. In many ways, this book is a tribute to all teachers like him. And what a beautiful moment, that while writing this book, my daughter Ana graduated from college as a history major. I give thanks to all the history teachers of my children, and I give gratitude for the history lessons my children have taught me—Ana, Maria, and Nico. Thank you for all your support to me over the years! And to my wife of over 25 years, Gaby: you have walked by my side through every trial and highlight. What a blessed, beautiful journey it has been! Without you, none of this is possible.

About the Authors

ART WORRELL is the Director of History for Uncommon Schools. Throughout his career, Art's teaching and coaching of other teachers have been featured in some of the most influential books in education, such as *Teach Like a Champion*, *Get Better Faster*, and *Leverage Leadership*. His 18-plus year career as a history teacher and instructional leader has included teaching and coaching both middle school and high school and designing rich curriculum and assessments. Art and his AP US History students achieved some of the highest results among urban schools and were featured in TNTP's "Room to Run" series as an example of what students can accomplish when presented with high expectations and rigorous work. In addition to his work at Uncommon Schools, Art has done adjunct work for the Relay Graduate School of Education. He holds a BA in history from Rutgers University and an MAT in education from the Relay Graduate School of Education.

PAUL BAMBRICK-SANTOYO is the founder and dean of the Leverage Leadership Institute, creating proof points of excellence in urban schools worldwide, as well as Chief Schools Officer for Uncommon Schools. Author of multiple books, including *Love & Literacy*, *Driven by Data 2.0*, *Leverage Leadership 2.0*, *Get Better Faster*, and *A Principal Manager's Guide to Leverage Leadership 2.0*, Bambrick-Santoyo has trained over 35,000 school leaders worldwide in instructional leadership, including at multiple schools that have gone on to become the highest-gaining or highest-achieving schools in their districts, states, and/or countries. Prior to these roles, Bambrick-Santoyo cofounded the Relay National Principal Academy Fellowship and led North Star Academies in Newark, New Jersey, whose academic results rank among the highest in urban schools in the nation.

Introduction: Make History

"History is not a set of facts but a series of arguments, issues, and controversies."

—James Loewen

"History has to be rewritten in every generation, because although the past does not change, the present does; each generation asks new questions of the past, and finds new areas of sympathy as it re-lives different aspects of the experiences of its predecessors."

—Christopher Hill

In 1963, the United States was on the cusp of tremendous change. For a country still reeling from the assassination of John F. Kennedy, Lyndon B. Johnson's ambitious social agenda was an opportunity for the nation to realize a dream that had been abruptly cut short. During the 11 months prior to the 1964 election, Johnson passed the landmark Civil Rights Bill and the Economic Opportunity Act, along with several notable others. Once elected, he launched the Great Society program, a large-scale social reform agenda that vastly expanded the government's role in alleviating the social and economic ills, the likes of which had not been seen since Roosevelt's New Deal.

For many students of history in the late 1960s, the Great Society looked to be a great success—it spawned programs like Head Start, Medicaid, and Medicare that still exist today. Yet as the years passed, the Great Society program found itself criticized on two fronts, by conservatives for increasing inflation and sparking an economic downturn and by liberals for being deprioritized in the tumult of the Vietnam War. It makes the curious historian wonder: What is the legacy of the Great Society? To what extent was the Great Society a success?

Scott Kern, a teacher of AP US History in Newark, New Jersey, brings this lesson to his class, which he adapted from the Stanford History Education Group. Let's see how they wrestle with it. We've included a transcript of part of the conversation. As you read, note what strikes you about the discussion. What does it say about how Scott teaches history?

Sample Class Discussion

Lesson Prompt: To what extent was the Great Society a success?

SCOTT (TEACHER): Okay, based on the evidence that you and your peers analyzed, was the Great Society a success? Tim, please start us off.

TIM: I think it's really hard to argue that it wasn't. Johnson's Great Society established some powerful programs that continue to combat poverty and improve the lives of Americans. Medicare and Medicaid are two programs that provide health insurance for the elderly and low-income Americans and both are still popular today.

SHANA: I agree with Tim. Johnson also started the Head Start program, and the data in source 3 show us how early childhood education intervention programs have huge positive effects on high school graduation rates. And that data from 2016 shows how the Great Society still benefits Americans.

MICHELLE: That doesn't even include the impact that the Great Society had on the expansion of Civil Rights. The Civil Rights Act of 1964 and the Voting Rights Act of 1965 are noted in source 4 by Califano, who states "the Voting Rights Act opened the way for Black Americans to strengthen their voice in every level of government."

[Scott charts these claims and evidence using the overhead projector.]

SCOTT (TEACHER): Well said. Really interesting ideas. So far no one has cited our 5th source [Dr. Martin Luther King's speech at Riverside Church] or our 6th [Gregory Schneider's critique of the long-term failures of the Great Society]. How do you reconcile those voices with your argument? Turn and talk with your partners.

[Scott circulates to listen to conversations. After 1 minute, he calls the class together.]

Scott (Teacher): What would you say?

Courtney: Dr. King would not agree with our argument about the success of the Great Society. At least not entirely.

Scott (Teacher): Why do you say that?

Courtney: Because in his speech at Riverside Church in 1967, Dr. King argued that the war in Vietnam drained the Great Society of the resources that it needed to really fight poverty. He saw the Vietnam War as an enemy of the poor. I think the Great Society was only successful in a limited way. It could have had an even greater impact if Johnson had not escalated the war in Vietnam.

Scott (Teacher): Darryl.

Darryl: I agree with Courtney that the Vietnam War limited the success of the Great Society. We see that idea also expressed in the 1967 Herbert Block political cartoon. Johnson gave everything to the Vietnam War while leaving the needs of urban America unaddressed.

Jay: I hear you, Darryl, but I think King is still on the side of seeing the value of the Great Society. He thinks it doesn't go far enough. As the leading figure in the Civil Rights movement, and someone who played a huge role in getting key legislation like the Civil Rights Act and the Voting Rights Act passed, King clearly wanted the government, and the Great Society, to do more to protect civil rights. I think Schneider's critique is different. Schneider argues that the Great Society's government welfare programs burdened state budgets without significantly reducing the poverty rate. I think we have to look at the impact, not just the intent.

Lucy: I'd love to see more statistics—on the economic impact and on the funding for the Great Society. How underfunded was it? I don't really know. But when I think about how long these programs have lasted—more than 50 years? That seems to outweigh your argument, Jay.

Scott (Teacher): Wow. Those are all powerful questions to consider. So we seem to have a few ideas emerging here. Could I have someone reframe our debate? To what extent was the Great Society a success?

Lucas: Well, Michelle and a few others have argued that the Great Society was a success due to the legacy of many of its programs that continue to shape America like Medicare, Medicaid, and the Head Start program. On the other hand, it could also be argued that the Great Society didn't do enough, or that the overspending negatively impacted our economy and caused more joblessness and poverty.

Hazel: Yeah, and we also talked about its impact on civil rights as an important part of its legacy.

Scott (Teacher): Well said. Thank you, Lucas and Hazel. Okay, everyone take a few moments to revisit your initial argument. Based on the evidence that we examined, to what extent was the Great Society a success? Write your thesis statement and the core evidence from at least two of our sources that you will use to defend it. And remember to acknowledge and address the counterarguments in your thesis. And as Lucy named, also consider what other types of sources you might want to examine to fully answer this question. Please begin.

Although this conversation appears ordinary on the surface, magic lies beneath it. Scott's students craft arguments using multiple perspectives and spar with one another to carefully shape their understanding of history. The work they do is more meaningful than memorizing a set of details or describing a key historical event. Instead of reciting history, Scott's students are piecing it together—source by source, event by event. By critically evaluating different perspectives to land on their own, they do something remarkable: they move from reciting history to making it.

Core Idea

Don't recite history; make it.

What makes Scott's classroom so special—and those of countless history teachers who carry on the same approach—is that students are invited to become historians as they strive to better understand the past. "Making history," or piecing together the past to give it meaning, unlocks the mystery of what came before. This historical sensemaking transforms the act of learning history from passive absorption to active, earnest intellectual work. Once students are able to do that, the past unfurls around them in all its richness and nuance.

In observing and teaching history across multiple decades, we have encountered many classroom discussions like the one seen in Scott's classroom: teachers who have created cathedrals of learning where students are able to learn, probe, acquire knowledge, and critique it. These classrooms radiate with the knowledge and habits of mind necessary to make informed judgments and make sense of the history presented to them. These spaces cultivate students' sense of self and inspire them with a focused emphasis on agency. History is not just about teaching the past. It's also about teaching students how to participate in the present with empathy and purpose to foster a vision for a better future.

But classroom experiences like Scott's aren't built in a day (neither was Rome for that matter). They take time, skillful effort, and the expert leveraging of the resources around them. Thus the nature of this book and our desire to write it.

We met each other back in 2005, when Art was in his first year as a middle school history teacher in Newark, New Jersey, and Paul was a superintendent. While in different places on our journeys, our shared passion for teaching led our paths to intersect—and we've worked as friends and colleagues ever since.

But the real seeds of this book were planted far earlier.

ART'S STORY

When I think back to the beginning of my journey as an educator, 17 years ago, I now realize that my "why" began long before that. My father passed away on January 26, 2020, after a long struggle with cancer. In the months before he died, he and I were working on his memoir. It was a way for us both to fight through the pain of that time, to bond. But now, I also realize it was part of a larger journey I had been on to learn who my father really was.

Growing up, I was deeply afraid of my dad. He was a man of few words with a tough exterior: a larger than life, muscle-bound cop who literally struck fear into my heart. As a kid, he was the disciplinarian that stepped in if my brother or I stepped too far out of line. In fact, the only time that he would really even begin to open up was when he would talk about his faith or when he preached from the pulpit on a Sunday morning. For most of my young life it was like that. My father—more myth than man. Always present, but never really within sight.

It wasn't until high school History, when I read James Baldwin's *The Fire Next Time* on my own that I started to unravel the mystery of my father. Baldwin reframes and retells the history of this country not from the perspective of the powerful, of the white oligarchy, but from the bottom up—the oppressed, disenfranchised, and often silenced. Through reading Baldwin I started exploring history in a new way, and it set me on a path to explore and learn for the first time about Cesar Chavez and the fight for the rights of migrant workers, about Ida B. Wells's work to stop the lynching of Blacks throughout the South, and about the harsh realities of life in the Jim Crow South–the same Jim Crow South that my father was born into in Como, North Carolina in 1946.

Learning about this history helped me see my past with new eyes. I finally understood why as a 5th-grader, I often had to help my dad decode certain words while he studied his Bible. Growing up in a segregated South, he watched white students take the bus to school while he and his brothers worked on a small peanut farm to help his family survive. This illuminated why, after he and his brothers migrated to the Bronx, New York, in the 1960s, my father chose to join the police academy. It was a move designed not only to escape poverty, but to support his community, which he did through an NYPD community engagement program that he ran in the South Bronx until his retirement. I also came to understand why he and my mother, despite their modest income, spent whatever they had to provide the best education that they could for my brother, sister, and me. As my knowledge and understanding of a more complex, nuanced, and inclusive history began to grow, my little world in the Bronx, and my father as an individual, suddenly started to make more sense. I could finally see my father in his wholeness: his scars, his fears, and his hopes and dreams for his community and his family.

This "why" has sustained me for the past 17 years. It is what rescues me from my most tired or cynical moments. It is my hope that as history teachers, we can help students experience the same revelatory moments that I did when I read Baldwin and so many others. And in understanding the past, perhaps our students too will understand and shape their own world for the better.

PAUL'S STORY

I was only 17 years old when I walked into a class that would teach me a lesson I would never forget. Donald Sprague was officially a Latin teacher, but I learned more about history in that class than in any other I took in high school. It was the late 1980s, and Central America was in the midst of civil wars and battles between largely military-led governments and guerilla forces. El Salvador was a prime example. On November 16, 1989, the Salvadoran army's elite counter-insurgent unit entered the residence of the rector of Central American University and murdered Ignacio Ellacuría, a Jesuit priest and the rector of the university, along with five other Jesuit priests, a caretaker, and her daughter. The unprecedented nature of the murders would attract international attention and be a turning point for a cease-fire and eventual settlement to the civil war.

When I walked into Latin class on November 17, I knew none of this. We had been in the midst of reading *The Iliad* in Latin, and had come to the final scenes where Achilles has gone through a conversion—where the savage anger that had driven so much of his military prowess converts to pain and later a humanizing self-recognition that would end in his own death at the hands of Paris. Mr. Sprague put the *New York Times* article in front of us and asked us to read it. I looked around, and the looks on my peers' faces confirmed that none of us knew why we were doing this. After a pause, he turned and asked us, "Tell me about the hero theory. Apply it to Achilles." After a few adequate responses, he asked, "Now apply it to today: tell me why hundreds of Jesuits today volunteered to immediately take the place of Ellacuría and his peers."

Our responses were somewhat feeble, as adolescents caught off guard are wont to be. But the message landed, at least for me. Looking back, it was a turning point in my life trajectory, well-timed to ignite the dreams of an idealistic youth. Yet it was also so much more. Reflecting back on that moment decades later, I can see the contours of excellent teaching, and also what moments like that can do to create a craving to learn from the past—from literature and history—to apply to today. Making sense of documents from the past, illuminated by the events of today, guided the way I thought about teaching and learning—and doing.

OUR STORY

It has been many years since these seminal experiences, and in the 17 years since we met, we've worked together to observe, collect, and teach the best practices of talented social studies and history teachers. In *Make History,* we share the teacher moves, practices, and systems that have transformed social studies and history classrooms from places of passive learning to ones of active exploration. This book isn't about "what to teach." Instead, we focus on how to teach, or more aptly, "What is a powerful approach to teaching history?" *Make History* is a practical guide to the teaching of history, one that honors disciplinary thinking, background knowledge, and classroom discourse in equal measure.

We developed this approach over years of study and with the help of some brilliant people in the world of education. Within these pages, we highlight insights from several of these colleagues for the way their thinking has shaped our work, namely Abby Reisman, Brenda Santos, Eric Foner, Grant Wiggins, Jay McTighe, James Verrilli, Jon Bassett, Gary Shiffman, Sam Wineburg, Sonia Nieto, and Zaretta Hammond. We combined their expertise with the firsthand knowledge and experience gained from observing and working alongside hundreds of talented, passionate social studies and history teachers. These educators excelled at transforming theory into practice, providing us with valuable information about the teaching moves that matter most in the classroom, as well as ways to make them bite-sized, actionable, and, most importantly—replicable.

Unlike the empire builders of Rome, most teachers don't have centuries at their disposal; an academic school year is the most we typically get. Nevertheless, with the appropriate tools there is much we can accomplish within a single school year. Read on to see what it takes.

A "PRACTICAL GUIDE": WHAT YOU'LL FIND IN THIS BOOK

The pages that follow are a concrete, step-by-step guide to awakening the historical thinker in every student.

Part 1: Define the Destination starts from the end game: What is the outcome we hope for from an engaging, rigorous history classroom? It lays out the blueprint of where we are headed in the construction of powerful history classrooms and describes all the steps necessary to teach a given lesson.

Part 2: Build Knowledge takes the blueprint and starts laying the foundation. Step-by-step, we break down the moves that teachers make to equip students with the knowledge they will need to do critical, disciplinary thinking and analysis.

Part 3: Grapple with Evidence details how to lead students through the weeds of history. Through authentic classroom case study, we show how teachers can create a worthwhile challenge within a given lesson, purposefully activating the knowledge that students need to navigate the challenge with minimal teacher support. We also share simple ways to track student understanding during independent work time. This real-time monitoring makes instruction responsive and immediate.

Part 4: Make Sense of It Through Discourse shows how to capitalize on a well-laid foundation as students apply their knowledge to make sense of history through enlightening discourse.

Part 5: Stamp and Measure the Learning closes out successful instruction with verbal and written records of key ideas, in addition to ways to formally assess student understanding over time. In Part 6: Put It All Together we do just that. Two connected sets of history lessons (one each for US and World History) show how to introduce essential historical context and story, foster productive struggle, and facilitate fruitful discourse.

With these materials, we construct our cathedral of learning. Yet none of these moves would be complete without the resources to make them happen. To illuminate the history classroom, we offer some key guides.

TURNING ON THE LIGHT: MAKING GOOD TEACHING VISIBLE

Teaching is challenging: the best ideas are challenged when standing in front of a group of young people who are pushing, stretching, and needing to be engaged differently every day. To make sure this book isn't theoretical, all of these ideas have been tested and tried across all grade spans and subjects. We bring these to life in videos and work samples.

See It: Videos and Work Samples

Videos

The best way to learn about teaching history is to see it in action. As such, *Make History* includes videos from real classrooms in grades 5–12. You will see authentic classroom interactions between teachers and students, and the lessons we can learn from them. Clips are indicated by this symbol:

WATCH Clip 4: Jillian Gaeta—An Engaging Opening Hook

Whenever possible, we recommend viewing each clip before reading the accompanying transcript and text. Although we strive to include the most meaningful aspects within the written description, watching those "a-ha" moments as they unfold is an experience unto itself.

Work Samples

Good teaching doesn't just happen—it's something teachers prepare for. To that end, we also show you the planning that teachers do to prepare for their classes: annotated lesson plans, tools to use in the classroom, etc. We've also included student work samples to illustrate what students can produce during and after effective history instruction.

Samples of Student/Teacher Work: Four-Corner Analysis

POV
Creole
elite independence
anti mercantilism

mercantilism HC
slavery, silvertrade
post-American Rev.
during Fr + Haitian Revs

SOURCE: Juan Pablo Viscardo, a Peruvian creole, "An Open Letter to America," 1791

Spanish restrictions on travel and commerce sealed America off from the rest of the world [limiting] our basic personal and property rights.... We in America are perhaps the first to be forced by our own government to sell our products at artificially low prices and buy what we need at artificially high prices. This is the result of the Spanish commercial monopoly system, combined with taxes and official fees....

...Spain could have left us the administration of our own affairs, one would think. Americans, being those most concerned by affairs of America, logically ought to fill the public offices of their own country for the benefit of all concerned. But that has been far from the case.

Audience
Creoles in Latin America

PURPOSE
Rally support for independence movement in Latin America

SS: LA. independence motivated by creoles' desire to control their own economic + political systems... Since Viscardo is a creole, he would likely have some economic means, and therefore be frustrated with Sp. mercantilism policies that stifled the potential profit of American-born creoles.

Name It: Core Ideas and One-Pagers

Seeing best practices is one thing. Naming them is another. While there are multiple ways to describe the same technique, if we use different terms, it is difficult to work together to get better. We use consistent language throughout the text to make it easier to share knowledge.

Core Ideas

These are the key ideas of each section. They simplify complex ideas into concise, sticky phrases.

> **Core Idea**
>
> Name the corners to frame the meaning.

Key Takeaways

At the end of each major part, a box recaps the core ideas we've discussed. Use it as a quick refresher or as a thumbnail to preview some of the section's contents:

> **Key Takeaways**
>
> High expectations are set not by what we say, but by what we expect—and what we accept—in student writing.

Stop & Jot

This book is an interactive experience. Use the Stop & Jot boxes to record your thoughts.

One-Pagers

Over the course of our work together, we have gathered history teachers from middle school and high school as well as professors from the university level to help us collectively shape a series of "one-pagers," brief guides that describe or illustrate key aspects of instruction. Think of these as the cheat sheets of the book: printer friendly and easy to carry around with you when teaching or planning for instruction. Here is a sample snippet from the Inquiry Lesson One-Pager.

Excerpt—Inquiry One-Pager

Guide Discourse
10-12 min
	Facilitate the Large Group Discourse
	• Strategically call on students
	   o Start with students who have more limited arguments
	• Maximize student talk:
	   o Volleyball, not ping pong: call on 2-3 students before responding
	   o Utilize universal prompts:
	      ■ "Build." "Elaborate." "Agree or disagree?"
	      ■ "How can you prove/corroborate this?" "Where do you find evidence for this?" "Other evidence?"
	      ■ "Are there other interpretations?"
	• Chart key arguments and evidence from students
	   o Ensure students take parallel notes

To make it easy for this book to live on for you long after you've finished reading it, you'll find a history handbook in the online appendix that consolidates all these guides into one place. The handbook includes teacher- and student-facing resources that you can use in class—everything from student reference sheets to classroom signage to tips for launching the lesson. We've organized it by chapter to make it easier to bring to life any new ideas you have after reading.

Do It: Materials to Make It Happen

With all these resources in hand, all that is left to plan is how to make it happen. We help you accomplish this by doing self-assessments throughout the text and then giving you structures to roll out new habits or skills and maintain them.

Self-Assessment

At the end of each major section, a self-assessment guides you through a reflection of your own school/classroom: What are the strengths and what are the areas to improve? All the habits and skills introduced in the chapter are listed within the box alongside a rubric score. Score yourself at the end of each chapter to help prioritize your next steps. (In Part 6, we combine these self-assessments into a comprehensive evaluation to look at your class/school as a whole.)

Self-Assessment Sample—Part 1

Part 1: Define the Destination	Score
• **Choose the Sources**	__/ 10
• Offer multiple perspectives of a historical actor, event, or development (e.g., dominant and overlooked voices, left- and right-leaning, etc.).	
• Manageable for the time that you have (one-page source per class period or four-paragraph-long sources).	
• **Design the Prompt and Exemplar Response**	__/ 10
• Prompt is clear and specific (4QM), compelling (relevant and thought-provoking), multifaceted (multiple possible answers), and manageable (doable in the time allotted).	
• Prompt addresses a key historical thinking skill.	
• Exemplar response sets the bar for what students should do to meet the task's demand.	
• Know-show chart names the knowledge and skills students need for the task.	
Part 1 Score:	____/20

Planning for Action

Once you've evaluated where you stand, you are ready to take action. This section, found at the end of each major part, helps you choose the most helpful resources included in the section and provides space to plan for potential modifications or adaptations.

Planning for Action Sample—Part 2

Planning for Action

• What resources from this section can you use to adjust your instruction? (You can find a print-ready version in the online materials.)

- How will you modify these resources to meet the needs of your class(es)?

Action	Date

Who Should Use This Book and How?

This book is for everyone who teaches history or coaches and influences its instruction. Our primary audience then, is middle school and high school social studies and history teachers. It's also designed for everyone who works with them: instructional coaches, department chairs, principals, curriculum directors, central office leadership, and any other staff who can affect the quality of learning for our students. The more that instructional leaders understand about the unique domain of history instruction, the more that they can support history teachers in bringing it to life.

Depending on your role, we recommend a few different pathways for reading this book:

- **New teachers:** If you are near the beginning of your teaching journey, welcome! We are excited to have you join this incredible community of fellow teachers. For you, we recommend reading from the beginning and following the chapters in order. To help ground you, think of an upcoming lesson or unit that you will be teaching (or would like to teach!) and use that as your anchor to plan each section. The first years are challenging for all of us, so we also recommend that you supplement this text with *Get Better Faster*, which breaks down the key classroom management techniques that can help in setting up your classroom for the first time. Also take note of the number of resources we mention in Part 1 to give you quick access to rich history materials if you don't yet have many at your disposal.

- **Experienced teachers:** If you have been teaching history for a while, you probably have a number of systems and habits already built into your classroom, as well as a comprehensive curriculum and sense of pacing throughout the year. In your case, select a key unit/set of lessons that you want to work on improving as you read the text. While you could choose one of your favorite lessons to keep perfecting it, we recommend picking a lesson/unit that has been more challenging or dry for you. *Make History* can help you find the gems of learning in that content and walk away with a reinvigorated unit that could have a ripple effect on the rest of your instruction. Start with Part 1 because without a clear bar that defines your goals, all the other practices will fall short, and then leverage Part 2 and Part 3 to cultivate the lessons that will lead to the peak of Part 4—rigorous discourse. Also make note of the real teaching vignettes throughout the text that could be directly transferrable to that content when you teach it yourself.

- **Department chairs and instructional coaches with a history background:** If you are a former history teacher who is now coaching, read this book with your own teaching in mind. How do the practices here give language to experiences you had yourself as a teacher? What new ideas could enhance your vision and ability to coach? Particularly take note of the "Key Takeaways" at the end of each section; these lay out a roadmap of key actions that you can use when coaching your teachers. You can also read this text with particular teachers in mind. Which teachers need support in which areas? You will find the materials are presented in a way to make it easy to turnkey into professional development for your department.

- **School leaders or coaches who are not former history teachers:** Although Art is a lifelong history teacher, Paul is not. One of Paul's "a-ha" moments as a principal and later superintendent was the subtle but important differences in best teaching practices across departments. While history supports and enhances literacy and has similarities to STEM courses, it is also quite distinct, and those differences are important. This book can enhance your ability to observe across different subjects (*Love & Literacy* can be a good companion text for seeing the similarities and differences with core English/literacy instruction).

- **Education professors:** To make this guide as practical as possible, we have focused on describing the key actions that effective teachers use in the classroom. All of these practices were honed through action research, and we've cited and given commentary in the end notes on the academic research that guided us. If you are using this text to teach pre-service teachers, we recommend assigning chapters and video viewing in chapter order. If you are teaching a specialized education course or working with more experienced teachers, assign the chapters in the order that best meets the needs of the course and your students. The discussion guide at the end of this book can be used to generate class conversations or for student reflection at the end of each part.

- **Anyone else with a love of history and its instruction:** Welcome! You have picked up this book to learn more about what makes great history instruction. As you read, pay close attention to the vignettes of actual classrooms, as well as the accompanying videos, and those will truly make the instruction come to life. And then apply as fits your role.

MAKING HISTORY—STARTING THE JOURNEY

Viewing the past through the perspective of today, it's likely that the students in Scott's class will have a different reading of the Great Society than many of the generations that came before. For one, they have the benefit of over 50 years of history to see the long-term impact of the program. And through the gift of readily accessible primary and secondary sources, they can also hear the diverse voices in the field and see the distinct stances each has taken on the legacy of the Great Society.

Why is this important to highlight? Although the past doesn't change, our understanding of it does.

Core Idea

The past doesn't change. How we understand it does.

The stories that we learn—or don't learn—about the past shape the present. So do our own perspectives and the context of the societies and times in which we live. That's why History class matters: it provides a deliberate and conscious entryway into the past. As students do the rigorous work of piecing together what came before, they learn to plumb the past for its depth, complexity, unresolved tensions, and hidden narratives. And in this space of sensemaking, historical empathy and critical thinking can be cultivated in tandem.

Great teaching doesn't just take into consideration what to teach; it also considers how and to whom. Knowing where we (and our students) stand in relation to the past plays a critical role in how and what we teach, so much so that Zaretta Hammond names awareness as a critical component to achieve rigorous learning.[1]

Our history students deserve—and require—both empathy and challenge. Together they make rigorous, long-term, independent learning possible—and it is this guiding principle that organizes *Make History*.

In the chapters that follow, we highlight what teachers do to connect students to the work of history: how they challenge, support, and engage them. Throughout it all, our focus remains centered on the most important outcome—inspiring our students to see history as deeply interwoven with the realities of today and the possibilities of tomorrow.

History class is preparation for life, and making sense of history is the work of every generation. Our charge as teachers is to show students how.

Core Idea

When we can make sense of the past, we can make history in the present.

Join us as we open the doors of the classroom to make history.

Define the Destination

"The stories a society tells about itself are a measure of how it values itself."
—Henry Giroux

"History is a people's memory."

—Malcolm X

Between 1775 and 1825, a series of revolutions swept across the Americas and Europe. The American War of Independence, the French Revolution, the Haitian Revolution, and multiple revolutions within Latin America reshaped the political landscape of the Western world. Across the Atlantic, elites born in the Americas chaffed at being governed by distant, aristocratic European rulers. Inspired by the ideals of the European Enlightenment, they declared themselves revolutionaries and took up the mantle of freedom. While the countries they founded were often grounded in Enlightenment principles, particularly the concept of individual freedom, only occasionally would these new countries live up to the promise of democratic rule.

The 11th-grade students in Jah'Nique Campos's World History class are in the middle of a unit on Latin American revolutions. Earlier in the week, they looked for connections between Enlightenment ideas and the Haitian Revolution. They now apply the same line of thinking to revolutions in the Spanish-speaking Americas to respond to Jah'Nique's inquiry question:

- To what extent were Latin American revolutions between 1775 and 1825 caused by Enlightenment ideas?

Join us as the debate begins.

Class Discussion

Lesson prompt:

To what extent were the Latin American revolutions between 1775 and 1825 caused by Enlightenment ideas?

JAH'NIQUE (TEACHER): Based on the evidence that you and your peers analyzed, and your knowledge of modern world history, to what extent were the Latin American revolutions caused by Enlightenment ideas? Taylor, Tommie, and Olu, please start us off.

TAYLOR: Well, based on these sources, I would definitely say that the Latin American revolutions were based in Enlightenment ideas. Viscardo, in his "Open Letter to America" discussed how personal and property rights were limited under the Spanish government, which sounds very similar to the ideas of John Locke.

TOMMIE: Agreed. Viscardo also talked about how the government controlled prices under what was a mercantilist policy. He also argued that Americans should have been left to their own governance, rather than be controlled by a distant power. That sounds very similar to the American Revolution and the arguments against the British government controlling its colonies across the Atlantic.

OLU: Wow, I couldn't disagree more! We have to contextualize these sources. Viscardo and Bolívar are creoles, mostly writing to a creole audience. Bolívar, in his Jamaica Letter, talked about how creoles were in a unique space between Europeans and Indigenous Americans. He actually said in the second to last paragraph, "In short, though Americans by birth we derive our rights from Europe, and we have to assert these rights against the rights of the natives, and at the same time we must defend ourselves against the invaders." Bolívar is literally arguing for creoles like himself to maintain their power over the Indigenous people. This isn't about natural rights. It's about a power grab!

[Multiple hands shoot up as students seem eager to jump in.]

JAH'NIQUE (TEACHER): That's a really interesting idea, Olu. Before others jump in, let's pause for a moment. What do we think about Olu's argument? If we contextualize these sources, where would we find more evidence to support Olu or to challenge his ideas? Turn and talk with your table partner to discuss.

[There's a notable buzz in the room as Jah'Nique circulates to listen in on conversations. Students flip through their notebooks and reference sheets as they discuss.]

JAH'NIQUE (TEACHER): Let's come together. [pauses] What do we think? What's happening at this time throughout the world and Latin America that might help us better understand these sources? Do we agree with Olu?

CHRIS: I think Olu's argument is really strong and I mostly agree. Bolívar is writing in the context of the Haitian Revolution, which was a successful rebellion of enslaved Black people against a European power. Compared against that, it's difficult to argue that Bolívar is calling for a revolution that is really concerned with natural rights.

RILEY: Exactly, Chris. And I would place the Haitian Revolution within the scope of all other Latin American revolutions. So, I think the question may be a bit flawed or too general. Which Latin American revolutions are we talking about? I think the Haitian revolution was way closer to reaching the ideals of the Enlightenment than Bolívar and the wars for independence in Colombia and Venezuela.

JAH'NIQUE (TEACHER): Well said. So as flawed as the question might be, how might we begin to answer it? And where would the fourth source—our only secondary source—fit into our argument? Turn and talk with your partner before we discuss as a whole group.

In a single class discussion, Jah'Nique's students do many remarkable things. They make connections between events, view evidence from multiple perspectives, and underscore important ideological debates that repeat throughout modern history. They are working together to place these revolutions within a larger historical context, that of a Western world considerably affected by new ideas about the power of the state and individual freedom. And Jah'Nique facilitates all of this without being the dominant voice in the room. Yet the resultant critical thinking didn't happen by chance or by the luck of a few students doing most of the work. Jah'Nique set the stage for this discourse to happen—not for a few, but for all students.

How did Jah'Nique think about teaching to make these times come alive for her students? She started by defining the destination.

Imagine you are planning a vacation. You have a few requirements: you know you are going to visit North Dakota, and you know you only have a week to do so, but beyond that the decisions are up to you as to how to spend that time. Teaching history is pretty similar. Most history curricula give us a general area of the historical "map" we have to cover: which time period, which geographies, which key historical events or figures. But that doesn't tell us how to get there. To determine her path, Jah'Nique treats her planning like a contemporary explorer: learn more about the area, finalize the destinations, and pack appropriately to get there. Without the destination, she wouldn't know how to move.

Core Idea

Instruction is rudderless without a destination.

Look back at Jah'Nique's lesson prompt.

Lesson Prompt

To what extent were the Latin American revolutions between 1775 and 1825 caused by Enlightenment ideas?

By choosing a provocative, focused prompt, Jah'Nique cuts a channel through the immense, choppy waters of revolutionary Latin America and offers students the chance to evaluate the events in depth. At its heart, that is what a proper destination does. It doesn't dictate what you should believe, only what you should be thinking about.

Core Idea

A proper destination doesn't dictate what you should believe,
only what you should be thinking about.

In the end, it's about the student making sense of that historical moment with their own defensible, plausible argument.

Jah'Nique didn't create this prompt out of thin air. It was the product of careful and deliberate planning. Let's unpack how she got there.

LEARN MORE—ENRICH YOUR HISTORY MAP
Craft Initial Questions

Take a moment and look at how Jah'Nique began her preparation for the lesson—she started with questions.

Initial Prompts for Jah'Nique's Class

- What does Viscardo's "An Open Letter to America" tell us about the root cause of revolution in Latin America?
- What was the impact of mercantilism on 18th-century Latin American revolutions?
- To what extent were the Latin American revolutions between 1775 and 1825 caused by Enlightenment ideas?
- Why did the Haitian Revolution begin in 1791?
- Given the circumstances at the time, were Viscardo and Bolívar right to fear a more radical revolutionary movement?

All of these prompts are convincing and plausible for a history class. One of the strengths they share is that they require students to make sense of history by analyzing and interpreting primary and secondary sources to construct an understanding of the past that takes into account the historic actors, intended audience, intended purpose, and the unique historical context of the time. In other words, while a bit broad in some instances, strong prompts ask students to do one or more of the following:

- Narrate: What happened?
- Interpret: What were they thinking?
- Explain: Why then and there?
- Judge: What do we think about that?

Jon Bassett and Gary Shiffman brought this understanding of history to life in their book *From Story to Judgment: The Four Question Method for Teaching and Learning Social Studies*. In their over 40 years of combined experience teaching history, Bassett and Shiffman came to understand that historians make sense of the past by asking a series of four questions, a process they call the Four-Question Method (4QM). The 4QM names the essential thinking steps that any historian takes when investigating the past. According to this method, the first step requires historians to create a narrative sketch of what happened. What was the actual timeline of events? Who were the key players? From there, historians seek to understand the motivations of these historical actors by asking, "What were they thinking?" This question is often best answered through a careful reading and analysis of primary sources. From there, historians try to contextualize the events of the past by asking "Why then and there?"[1] By examining the unique historical circumstances of a given time, historians can begin to explain why a particular phenomenon occurred in the way it did, in the specific time and place that it did. As Stanford professor and historian Sam Wineburg has said, by placing historical events within a specific and unique historical context, we help bridge the gap between the "strangeness of the distant past and familiarity of the human condition."[2] However, while the first three questions promote authentic historical thinking, they could be taught as surface-level academic exercises. Question 4, "What do we think about that?" deepens the thinking.[3] It requires student historians to weigh the decisions of historical actors and to make judgments about them, taking into account student perspectives and the limitations we have in ever truly "knowing" the past.

The beauty of Bassett and Shiffman's 4QM framework is that most of the questions we want to ask in History class are already one of the 4QM questions in disguise, although often worded more broadly or pointedly. Take Jah'Nique's original brainstormed prompts. Where would they fall in the 4QM framework? Here's how Jah'Nique categorizes them.

Potential Prompts for Jah'Nique's Class—A Case Study

Jah'Nique's Original Prompts	Corresponding 4QM Type
What was the impact of mercantilism on 18th-century Latin American revolutions?	Question 1: What happened?
What does Viscardo's "An Open Letter to America" tell us about the root cause of revolution in Latin America?	Question 2: What were they thinking?

Jah'Nique's Original Prompts	Corresponding 4QM Type
Why did the Haitian Revolution begin in 1791?	Question 3: Why then and there?
To what extent were the Latin American revolutions between 1775 and 1825 caused by Enlightenment ideas?	Question 2 or Question 3: (Dependent on the evidence curated to help respond to this question)
Given the circumstances at the time, were Viscardo and Bolívar right to fear a more radical revolutionary movement?	Question 4: What do we think about that?

The 4QM is a powerful tool to distill the actual thinking students need to do, define the depth at which they need to think to formulate historically defensible arguments, and help teachers generate more precise questions.

Generating these initial questions is only the starting point of planning. They lead directly to Jah'Nique's subsequent question: Where can she find information to help her—and her students—answer these questions?

In the end, the quality of your question will only be as good as the quality of the evidence you have to address it.

> ## Core Idea
>
> The quality of your class prompt will only be as good as the quality of the evidence you have to address it.

So how does Jah'Nique collect quality evidence for her students in order to create such a rich discussion?

Seek Sources with Multiple Perspectives

In the modern era of technology and information sharing, acquiring historical sources (both primary and secondary) about nearly any time period in history is easier than it has ever been. The new challenge lies in determining which sources to use and how to ensure their quality. The Stanford History Education Group (SHEG) has been the trailblazer to address this with its academic approach to source curation. Their *Read Like a*

Historian curriculum features vetted sources across multiple perspectives. You'll note their influence throughout our work.

Take Scott's Great Society lesson, adapted from SHEG.[4] Two of the sources he read to prepare are next. What do you notice? Why do you think these sources resonated with Scott?

Two Readings of The Great Society

Document 1

Source: Joseph A. Califano Jr., "What Was Really Great About the Great Society," *Washington Monthly*, 1999. (Excerpt)

■ ■ ■

If there is a prize for the political scam of the 20th century, it should go to the conservative for [claiming that the] Great Society programs of the 1960s were a misguided and failed social experiment that wasted taxpayers' money.

Nothing could be further from the truth. In fact, from 1963 when Lyndon Johnson took office until 1970 as the impact of his Great Society programs were felt, the portion of Americans living below the poverty line dropped from 22.2 percent to 12.6 percent, the most dramatic decline over such a brief period in this century. . . If the Great Society had not achieved that dramatic reduction in poverty, and the nation had not maintained it, 24 million more Americans would today be living below the poverty level . . .

Since 1965 the federal government has provided more than a quarter of a trillion dollars in 86 million college loans to 29 million students, and more than $14 billion in work-study awards to 6 million students. Today nearly 60 percent of full-time undergraduate students receive federal financial aid under Great Society programs . . .

Head Start has served more than 16 million preschoolers in just about every city and county in the nation and today serves 800,000 children a year . . . Lyndon Johnson knew that the rich had kindergartens and nursery schools; and he asked, why not the same benefits for the poor?

Is revolution too strong a word? Since 1965, 79 million Americans have signed up for Medicare. In 1966, 19 million were enrolled; in 1998, 39 million. Since 1966, Medicaid has served more than 200 million needy Americans. In 1967, it served 10 million poor citizens; in 1997, 39 million . . . Closely related to these health programs were efforts to reduce malnutrition and hunger. Today, the Great Society's food stamp program helps feed more than 20 million men, women, and children in more than 8 million households. Since it was launched in 1967, the school breakfast program has provided a daily breakfast to nearly 100 million schoolchildren.

The Voting Rights Act of 1965 . . . opened the way for black Americans to strengthen their voice at every level of government. In 1964 there were 79 black elected officials in the South and 300 in the entire nation. By 1998, there were some 9,000 elected black officials across the nation, including 6,000 in the South . . .

Document 2

Source: Gregory L. Schneider, Emporia State University, Bill of Rights Institute, "Life, Liberty and the Pursuit of Happiness." (Excerpt)

■ ■ ■

The Great Society and War on Poverty caused two interrelated problems. First, they led to increased dependency on government and perverse incentives that have hurt the poor. One example of this is welfare payments to single mothers that provided a disincentive for having a father in the home (benefits are cut if there is a working male member of the household). This led to a stark increase in single-parent households. Despite how heroic a single parent may be in trying to raise a child, the number of single-parent households in poverty increased drastically from 1.5 million in 1960 to approximately 5 million currently. This is compared with approximately 2 million married households under the poverty line, which has been constant since 1964. The continued fragmentation of families in poverty has led to increased crime, drug use, school dropout rates, and vast social problems in urban and rural America.

A second problem has been the cost of federal programs to aid the poor. Taxpayers have spent $20 trillion since the mid-1960s to fight the war on poverty. This includes housing allowances, food stamps, welfare payments, education, health care, and other benefits. The cost is more than the cost of all the wars fought in American history from the Revolution to the present day. What have been the results of such spending? The poverty rate has not declined and remains the same as in 1964, and there has been an explosion in the amount of federal dollars (and state dollars) needed to fund all the programs. The resulting entitlement crisis (especially for Medicare and Medicaid) threatens to bankrupt the country as states spend an increasing amount of their budgets on education and health care spending for the poor.

The demise of urban communities as a result of the war on poverty has also been a constant problem. Deindustrialization and the decline of entry-level jobs in industry occurred at the same time the federal government was moving in as a support network for poor people. Generational poverty expanded among the urban poor, who were increasingly segregated in failed schools, public housing, and a system that forced them into dependency. This is clearly seen in urban areas where blight, social problems, crime, and drug use are prevalent.

Stop & Jot

What strikes you about these two sources? Why were they valuable for Scott?

_____

_____

_____

These arguments offer two different but historically defensible arguments of the Great Society programs. In that sense, they both "work." Yet they also do something else: they keep Scott from analyzing history from a single perspective.

One of the biggest problems in modern-day society is the creation of echo chambers in which individuals read information only from a single perspective. Accelerated by social media search algorithms and polarized media outlets, people are often completely entrenched in a single worldview.

Without searching for a multitude of perspectives, teachers like Scott run the risk of bringing that same limitation into their classroom, and in doing so, oversimplifying history. They also won't be able to anticipate the differing views that might surface in their classrooms. Every additional argument Scott discovers affects his work in the same way: they root him in the disciplinary thinking of historians and prepare him to facilitate a class that takes all into account. In doing so, Scott gets to re-experience the joy of learning more about history himself—and the teaching becomes even more personally enriching!

Core Idea

You eliminate the echo chamber by actively seeking the counterargument.

Sparring with alternative arguments about a given historical event or phenomenon is a time-honored practice of historical thinking. Boxers spar when they practice their skills with other boxers. Yet sparring is not the same as fighting, for the goal is not to win—it's to get better. The same holds true for teachers. Sparring lays bare Scott's analysis, uncovering the holes in the evidence he may have used to support his initial argument and where the argument itself needs sharpening. As Scott spars, his thinking gets sharper, and his preparation smarter. You raise the bar when you spar with alternative perspectives.

You might find you have sparring partners among your fellow teachers in the same school with you. But whether you do or not, you can always look beyond the school walls to find a sparring partner, and who better to spar with than the great historians and thinkers of our time? You'll undoubtedly find something valuable to add to your analysis—and your joy of teaching.

Quick Resources for Finding Sources

Rachel Blake, a former HS World History teacher and current History Curriculum writer (you'll meet her in more depth in Part 2), loves to immerse herself in the latest scholarship. Even if it's a course that she's taught multiple times, she never considers her learning "done." New scholarship is always being published, and Rachel is always challenging herself to grow as a history teacher. The sources listed here have been the most useful to her curriculum development. May these resources be helpful to you as well.

- **Stanford History Education Group:** As mentioned earlier, this is the go-to site for high-quality, free lesson resources that are rooted in deep historical thinking. Documents are diverse, excerpted to be manageable in a given history lesson and centered on provocative history inquiries.
- **The OER Project:** Free, adaptable standards-aligned history courses for grades 6–12.
- **History podcasts:** On Top of the World (World History), Uncivil, and 1619 (US History) are good starting places.
- **Bancroft Award winners:** This is the most prestigious award for new historiography in American history. Consult the published list of winners for texts that could supplement your class.
- **American Historical Association:** A subscription to this publication keeps you in the loop about recent and well-regarded books in the field of history.
- **Jstor:** This digital database provides access to academic and scholar journals. Searching by topic can lead to valuable sources.
- **Online college syllabi:** Review posted syllabi for history courses at universities well-known for their history programs.
- **Robert Strayer's *Ways of the World* textbook:** This high-quality history textbook can supplement topics that don't have plentiful, interesting secondary sources.
- **Released College Board DBQ tasks:** In addition to providing quality, excerpted sources, released DBQ tasks give real insight into the types of tasks and thinking that College Board and the AP course require. It also ensures alignment of content and skill.
- **Choices Program:** Brown University offers an inquiry-based curriculum for history and current events courses. Its role-play approach is particularly effective for 9th and 10th grades.
- **Newspapers:** Rachel reads online newspapers, like the *New York Times*, and saves articles related to world and US History to reference for later use.
- **Your personal college book collection:** Rachel has kept many of the books from undergraduate and graduate history courses. She recommends taking notes on the blank pages in the back of the major or interesting topics, along with page numbers, to make the material easier to find later.
- **Colleagues in the history field:** If you have a network of colleagues in various areas of education (high school, college, graduate school), tap them for new resources and research.

- **Recommendation from experienced teachers:** Tap your network of experienced World History and US History teachers for ideas.
- **Librarians:** Ask your school and/or local librarians for help in sourcing materials. In addition, many large systems, like the Library of Congress and university libraries, allow you to submit free online queries to their staff and receive responses by email.

Jah'Nique consulted a number of the resources listed here to write her Latin American Revolutions lesson. Having increased her own personal knowledge of the historical period and different arguments, she is ready to determine the destination for her lesson. Let's see how she does so.

FINALIZE THE DESTINATION

Let's return to the final prompt that Jah'Nique chose for her lesson plan and compare it to the initial prompts that she originally generated for this lesson.

Craft a Class Prompt

Jah'Nique's Final Lesson Prompt

- To what extent were the Latin American revolutions between 1775 and 1825 caused by Enlightenment ideas?

Initial Prompts for Her Class

- What does Viscardo's "An Open Letter to America" tell us about the root cause of revolution in Latin America?
- What was the impact of mercantilism on 18th-century Latin American revolutions?
- To what extent were the Latin American revolutions between 1775 and 1825 caused by Enlightenment ideas?
- Why did the Haitian Revolution begin in 1791?
- Given the circumstances at the time, were Viscardo and Bolívar right to fear a more radical revolutionary movement?

Jah'Nique used a simple thought process to craft the final prompt: she took the core topic and gave it purpose.

Core Idea

Make your lesson engaging by giving your prompt multidirectional purpose.

History itself isn't automatically attractive to many students. But making judgments is the essence of adolescence. The phrase "To what extent" makes explicit that there is a continuum of plausible, defensible arguments, which keeps students from narrowing in on one or two possible answers. Comparison among revolutions in Latin America also makes the prompt more provocative: Why not compare revolutions across the Atlantic world to make students think twice about whether these movements are truly different or perhaps more similar than initially considered? (Riley raised this very point during discourse!) Comparing multiple revolutions incentivizes students to recognize trends over time and space, retrieve previously taught knowledge, make meaningful connections, and grapple with a question and task similar to those that they will see on high-stakes tests like the AP World History exam.

A Note to Consider—Strong Prompts Are Necessary but Insufficient

While Jah'Nique's final prompt is high quality, it won't automatically guarantee deep historical thinking. How she teaches it will. If Jah'Nique were to simply give a lecture of her own argument on the topic and ask students to regurgitate that response in an essay, there would be little to no rigor. In other words, while the question itself matters, the context in how the question is taught determines the value of the lesson (more on that in Parts 2 and 3).

A quality prompt can give the past purpose, transforming the process for students from being passive learners to active investigators.

Strong prompts feature the following:

Components of a Strong Prompt

- Clear and specific (4QM):
    - Narrate: What happened?
    - Interpret: What were they thinking?
    - Explain: Why then and there?
    - Judge: What do we think about that?
- Compelling:
    - Relevant and thought-provoking
    - Fits within a larger framework of global citizenship
    - Instills care and enthusiasm from teacher and students
- Multifaceted:
    - Multiple potential arguments that are historically defensible
- Manageable:
    - Accomplishable within the confines of a lesson, series of lessons, or unit of study
    - Students able to answer the question using readily accessible evidence

Take a moment and apply these skills to the act of generating a compelling prompt. What follows are a series of good-enough prompts that could be enhanced by these principles. Revise each one with the principles given. After you've taken a crack at it, turn the page and compare your revisions to the prompts we generated. (Note: there is no one right answer; it is the act of thinking about them and sparring with others that makes us stronger!)

Stop & Jot—Revising Prompts

Stop & Jot

Revise each of the following prompts, using your criteria:
- ☐ **Clear and specific (4QM)**
- ☐ **Compelling**
- ☐ **Manageable**
- ☐ **Multifaceted**

- How has modern history been shaped by Westernization?
  Revision:
  _____
  _____
  _____

- What was the impact of Reconstruction on US history?
  Revision:
  _____
  _____
  _____

- What were the causes of the Stono Rebellion?
  Revision:
  _____
  _____
  _____

STOP: Possible answers are on the next page. Don't move forward until you are ready!

Revising Prompts—Answer Key

Compare your revisions to the prompts we generated. There is no one right answer; use these simply to spar with your own (and send us your proposed prompts as we'd love to enrich our own practice as well!). Remember: it is the act of thinking about them and sparring with others that makes us stronger.

Three Revised Prompts

- Has modern history been shaped more by "Southernization" or "Westernization"?
- To what extent did Reconstruction secure and expand the rights of African Americans living in the South between 1865 and 1900?
- Why did the Stono Rebellion occur in 1739 in South Carolina?

Generating a prompt is the first step. Even more important is what it takes to answer it.

Create Exemplar Responses

Jah'Nique wrote the following exemplar arguments. What do you notice?

Lesson Prompt

To what extent were the Latin American revolutions between 1875 and 1825 caused by Enlightenment ideas?

Jah'Nique's Exemplar Responses

1. While the Latin American revolutions were framed in the language of Enlightenment ideas like popular sovereignty and natural rights, ultimately, creole revolutionary leadership was principally concerned with the preservation of their power over the native and African majority, and therefore failed to establish natural rights for all Latin American peoples.

2. While the Latin American revolutions were limited in their fulfillment of Enlightenment ideas, notable in the lack of substantive change in the nature of governance, the Enlightenment ideas were a fundamental rallying point and philosophy that mobilized people to stand with the revolutionaries against European rule.

In taking time to write these, Jah'Nique was not trying to determine one correct answer—far from it. Rather, she wanted to go through the same process she would ask of her students, and in the process, set the floor for what she wants students to accomplish.

Writing a response allows Jah'Nique to say, "I want all my students to reach this level of argumentation and analysis (the floor). While they might choose a different thesis and they might exceed the quality of my analysis, here is the baseline level of sophistication I am looking for." In the end, our curriculum expectations are meaningless until we define how our students will be assessed. As we shared in *Driven by Data 2.0*, the end product determines the bar for rigor. The exemplar response is the starting point for instruction, not the end.

> ### Core Idea
>
> The exemplar response is the starting point for instruction, not the end.
> It determines the bar for rigor.

What we expect our students to produce as a result of our teaching is the real bar that is established in our class. Nowhere is this more important than in extended written responses. We could have the same quality prompt, but if one teacher accepts an answer that has a simple thesis, poor analysis, and limited citation, that classroom is far less rigorous than one with higher expectations for argumentation and analysis. And those higher expectations are measured not in what we say but what we accept in student writing.

> ## Core Idea
> High expectations are not set by what we say, but by what we expect—and what we accept—in student writing.

Jah'Nique went far beyond the bulleted list or a jot of big ideas in her organizer; she wrote comprehensive arguments. Taking the time to write fully fleshed out responses prior to thinking about instruction opens a lens into what students will need to do to get there. By walking the road before her students, Jah'Nique cuts a path through the thicket, noting the alternative pathways, false trails, and rocky roads that students will likely encounter as they navigate. She knows she cannot guide the voices in the classroom unless she's traveled the path herself.

Prepared with greater clarity about the type of thinking students will do within a given lesson, Jah'Nique can now chart the path: determine what students will need in order to take the journey themselves.

CHART THE PATH

Step back for a moment and think about everything you have to do to be able to answer a prompt like Jah'Nique's: research different sources, contextualize them, and apply your previous knowledge to understand and analyze them. Jah'Nique takes the same approach with her students, starting with curating her sources.

Choose Your Sources

Reading historical sources serves two very important purposes for a student: it gives them multiple perspectives and it builds their knowledge. Let's unpack each.

Expose Them to Multiple Perspectives

As you know, there are more sources on a historical topic than students will ever have the time to read in class. Before teaching the lesson, Jah'Nique needs to determine which sources to put in the hands of her students, which will directly influence how students will view the past.

Consider, for example, two hypothetical lists of sources for Jah'Nique's lesson on Latin American revolutions. What pathway does each offer its students?

Two Possible Lists of Sources—Latin American Revolutions

List of Sources 1	List of Sources 2
• "Spanish-American Wars of Independence," *Encyclopedia Britannica* • A portrait of Simón Bolívar from 1827 • A map of colonies in Latin America on the eve of revolution, *Rise of the Spanish-American Republics*, 1921 • "The Other Revolution—Haiti," John Carter Brown Library	• Juan Pablo Viscardo, Peruvian creole, "An Open Letter to America," 1791 • Simón Bolívar, "Message to the Congress of Angostura; the congress was summoned by Bolívar during the wars of independence of Colombia and Venezuela in 1819 • "Discovering the Constitution of Cadiz," American Library of Congress • Simón Bolívar, "Jamaica Letter," written in 1815 to English colleague after several military defeats forced him into exile in Jamaica • Leslie Bethell, historian of Latin America, *The Independence of Latin America*, 1987 • Toussaint Louverture, excerpt from "Saint-Domingue Constitution," 1801 • Proclamation of Haiti's Independence by the General in Chief, Jean-Jacques Dessalines, to the Haitian people in Gonaives, on 1 January 1804

Stop & Jot

What pathway does each set of sources offer its students?

_____

_____

_____

Both lists of sources have rigorous, challenging texts that will stretch students, and both provide knowledge of the time period. So what are the differences? The perspectives they seek and the knowledge they build.

Take the first list. While they certainly are informative texts, they are still very limited to 20th-century secondary sources (*Britannica* and John Carter Brown Library), textbook-style readings that basically do the thinking for the students. Moreover, the included map and photo, while primary sources, do little to help a student advance their argument. If they read this list, it will be difficult to come up with multiple plausible arguments without doing outside research. List 2 is far more robust: not only do students hear directly from primary sources but also they hear multiple perspectives. The sources range from the imperial power (Spain—Constitution of Cadiz) to lead revolutionaries (Bolívar and Viscardo).

When gathering sources, Jah'Nique's focus is not on finding the most "right" or "complete" ones. It is about curating a selection of sources robust enough to talk to— and spar with—each other.

Core Idea

Select a set of sources that enable students to talk to—and spar with—each other.

Selecting sources from multiple angles is more easily said than done. Here are some guiding questions that Jah'Nique uses to help her choose:

- Are both dominant and marginalized voices of that time represented?
- Are there both traditionally conservative and liberal perspectives (or whatever were the prevailing different perspectives of that time period/era)?
- Do these sources consider both top-down and bottom-up historical perspectives?
- Do the sources disagree with each other on why/what/how it happened?
- Do these sources grapple with historiography on the topic?

By following these prompts, Jah'Nique is acknowledging that every source has a perspective (and a bias), and she needs to step outside of her own perspective to make sure that she is not transmitting only that perspective to students. When Jah'Nique presents a mix of sources pulled from multiple angles, she complicates and deepens analysis for her students—and for herself. As each new voice is added, what students can take away from the story of revolutionary Latin America becomes richer and more nuanced.

By preserving traditional narratives and sources and also widening the lens to include additional perspectives, we avoid the danger in flattening the past to a single story. With only one perspective, we lose history's complexity, and with it, the stories of the people most likely to have their stories forgotten or erased. In losing that complexity, we also lose the natural tension that can excite students so completely. What better way to engage adolescents than let them debate? That is the heart of the discipline of history.

Sourcing widely enriches our teaching in other ways. Different sources not only provide students with different historical perspectives but also they can provide vital schema.

Excerpting Documents

It is important to carefully manage the length and number of sources that you have students read and analyze within a single lesson. Remember, the goal of an inquiry-based lesson is not to spend all class reading the texts. A strong inquiry-based lesson also pushes students to contextualize sources, place them in conversation with each other, and corroborate and synthesize evidence to make sense of the past. That is rigorous work, and students need time to be able to deeply analyze evidence and discuss their findings in a meaningful way. Given the complexity of most primary and scholarly secondary sources, consider the following guidelines that we have culled from SHEG's guidance and tested with our own years of experimentation in the classroom:[5]

- For close reading of a single document, excerpt the text to be about a page in length.
- If inquiry requires using multiple sources from multiple perspectives, excerpt the sources to be about a paragraph and limit sources to four or fewer.
- If the topic and question require an examination of a text longer than a page or more than four sources, assign some or all as pre-work.
- If students need to work with a greater number of texts, consider collaborative reading activities. Visit https://www.edutopia.org/topic/collaborative-learning for more.

Build Student Knowledge

Here's a snippet from one of Jah'Nique's sources, Simón Bolívar's "Message to the Congress of Angostura," an 1819 congress convened by Bolívar during the wars of independence in Colombia and Venezuela. What knowledge can you glean from this reading?

Acquire Knowledge—Case Study

Read the following source. What knowledge can you glean from this reading? What additional knowledge do you need to understand it?

■ ■ ■

Source: Simón Bolívar, "Message to the Congress of Angostura," 1819.

■ ■ ■

We are not Europeans; we are not Indians; we are but a mixed species of aborigines and Spaniards.

Americans by birth and Europeans by law, we find ourselves engaged in a dual conflict: we are disputing with the natives for titles of ownership, and at the same time we are struggling to maintain ourselves in the country that gave us birth against the opposition of the invaders. Thus our position is most extraordinary and complicated. But there is more. As our role has always been strictly passive and political existence nil [zero], we find that our quest for liberty is now even more difficult to accomplish; for we, having been placed in a state lower than slavery, had been robbed not only of our freedom but also of the right to exercise an active domestic tyranny . . . We have been ruled more by deceit than by force, and we have been degraded more by vice than by superstition. Slavery is the daughter of darkness: an ignorant people is a blind instrument of its own destruction. . . .

Stop & Jot

What knowledge can you glean from this reading? What additional knowledge do you need to understand it?

_____
_____
_____
_____

Bolívar's speech is a powerful source in offering the view of creole protest at a time when American-born (creole) elites had grown disenchanted with overseas rule. But it also does more than that: it enables students to acquire knowledge.

The source line introduces a prominent figure of the time: the creole Simón Bolívar. His speech invokes the social hierarchy of the time, with powerful European leaders at the top, creoles beneath them, and the Indigenous at the bottom. His group, he declared, was embattled on both sides. Europe denied them full liberty while the Indigenous population agitated for land ownership. Bolívar argued that something must be done to free these elites from a state he hyperbolically compares to enslavement. While Bolívar's message to congress does not teach all of the knowledge necessary to respond to the prompt in full, the slice of historical context it provides makes a nice dent and arms students with more.

The power of reading historical sources isn't just to illuminate perspective—students also gain knowledge. That keeps teachers from doing all the lectures of a traditional class. And in guiding students to build their own knowledge, they become smarter. (Note: it's true that you can't find all the knowledge students will need from a limited number of sources. In Part 2: Build Knowledge, we show how to build additional knowledge to help students keep the bigger historical picture in mind.)

By choosing her sources, Jah'Nique has equipped students with the key pit stops on the journey of historical analysis. Now she considers the thinking skills it will take to unpack them.

Identify the Historical Thinking Skills

Part of what makes History such a rich discipline is the range of thinking skills that can be applied to any time period. Many organizations have created a list of disciplinary thinking skills that can serve as a guide for teaching and cultivating historical thinking in your students. The lists are largely similar; just pick one and stick with it to create a common language for your students. Jah'Nique uses the College Board's Advanced Placement History framework because it exposes students to all the types of disciplinary thinking they would be expected to know for college-level History coursework. The AP History's list of historical thinking skills appears next. (The fifth thinking skill, making connections, refers to the underlying reasoning processes of comparison, continuity or change over time, and causation.)

Historical Thinking Skills

The College Board[6]

1. **Development and Processes:** the ability to identify and explain a historical concept, development, or process.

2. **Sourcing and Situation:** Identify and explain a source's point of view, purpose, historical situation, and/or audience. Explain the significance of a source's point of view, purpose, historical situation, and/or audience, including how these might limit the use(s) of a source.

3. **Claims and Evidence in Sources:** Identify and describe a claim and/or argument in a source. Identify the evidence used in a source to support an argument. Compare the

arguments or main ideas of two sources. Explain how claims or evidence support, modify, or refute a source's argument.

4. **Contextualization:** Identify and describe a historical context for a specific historical development or process. Explain how a specific historical development or process is situated within a broader historical context.

5. **Making Connection:** Identify patterns among or connections between historical developments and processes. Explain how a historical development or process relates to another historical development or process.

6. **Argumentation:** Make a historically defensible claim. Support an argument using specific and relevant evidence. Use historical reasoning to explain relationships among pieces of historical evidence. Corroborate, qualify, or modify an argument using diverse and alternative evidence in order to develop a complex argument.

Over time, Jah'Nique makes sure to address all the thinking skills across various lessons and units. In the case of this lesson, comparison is the primary skill. But so many of these skills can be brought to fruition by the simple act of unpacking a source.

"Source" Your Sources

One of the breakthrough moments in our journey to writing this book was a day when two leaders from higher education came to observe History teaching with us: Joel Breakstone, director of the Stanford History Education Group, and Eric Shed, who at the time was the director of Harvard's Teacher Fellows program. One of the observations was of Art's own AP US History class. The lesson was a powerful one: Art's students were analyzing a speech by the founder of the Ku Klux Klan. As we observed together, the 11th-graders were making very thoughtful statements analyzing the substance of the speech. They noted the white supremacist doctrine that dominated the speech and also unpacked the subtle imagery that reinforced the group's hatred. They noted how the founder's beliefs clouded and shaded everything he said. In all, it was a high-quality class discussion.

As we walked out of the class, we were proud of our students and the level of analysis they had done. Paul turned to Joel and Eric and asked them their opinion. They complimented the quality of the habits of discourse and the student-driven discussion. But then Joel said the following, "But they didn't source the document."

At first, Paul was taken aback. Didn't they see how the students were able to unpack the bias of the author and the way in which white supremacy permeated their arguments? Joel responded, "Yes, that is important. But what they didn't note was the timing of this speech. This was the founding speech of the KKK when multiple white supremacist organizations were competing for membership and power. The audience of his speech wasn't the general white population. He was trying to recruit members of other white supremacist organizations to come under his authority. That is the context for this speech; and that is what it would mean to 'source' the document."

In that moment, we deepened our understanding of historical thinking. It's not enough to unpack the content. Contextualize it to fully unpack its meaning.

Core Idea

"Source" the document: contextualize its content to unpack its meaning.

What is an easy way to do this? Think about four corners.

Annotate Four Corners

Walk into Jah'Nique's classroom during this unit, and at one point you will note that her students are reading "An Open Letter to America" by Juan Pablo Viscardo, a

---

Four Corners: "An Open Letter to America"

POV
Creole
elite
pro-independence
anti mercantilism

mercantilism — HC
slavery, silver trade
Post-American Rev.
during Fr + Haitian Revs

SOURCE: Juan Pablo Viscardo, a Peruvian creole, "An Open Letter to America," 1791

Spanish restrictions on travel and commerce sealed America off from the rest of the world [limiting] our basic personal and property rights…. We in America are perhaps the first to be forced by our own government to sell our products at artificially low prices and buy what we need at artificially high prices. This is the result of the Spanish commercial monopoly system, combined with taxes and official fees….

…Spain could have left us the administration of our own affairs, one would think. Americans, being those most concerned by affairs of America, logically ought to fill the public offices of their own country for the benefit of all concerned. But that has been far from the case.

PURPOSE
Rally support
for independence
movement in
Latin America

Audience
Creoles in Latin America

SS: LA. independence motivated by creoles' desire to
control their own economic + political systems…
Since Viscardo is a creole, he would likely have some
economic means, and therefore be frustrated with Sp.
mercantilism policies that stifled the potential profit of
American-born creoles.

Peruvian creole. As you walk around, you see that one student has annotated her documents in the following way. What strikes you about her annotations?

Stop & Jot

What is the value of this student's annotations?

_____

_____

_____

At each corner, the student has written a pivotal piece of information about the source that will help her better understand it. Art and his peers call this *four-corner annotation*, and although its origin is unknown, this strategy has become a handy way to teach students to historically unpack a text.

Primary sources are the beating heart of a history class; they bring the past to life. But before students can grapple with their content, they must first contend with the context of their creation. Who wrote the source and what was their point of view? What is the historical context in which this was written? To whom were they speaking? What was their purpose? And the final annotation (labeled as *SS* on the student work) is the Significance statement. Why does this matter? And what is its significance in connection to the prompt?

Just like a picture frame focuses the viewer on the image, four corners bring out the meaning of the text.

Core Idea

Name the corners to frame the meaning.

Read for Significance—Four-Corner Annotation

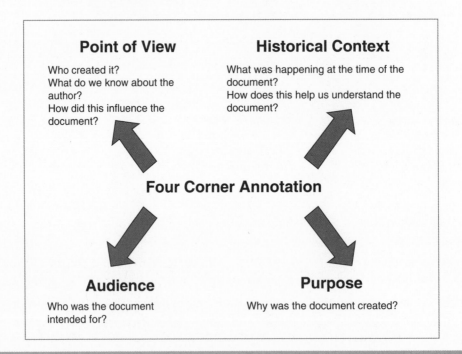

These are critical components for students to consider before reviewing the source itself. But these are not instinctual.

Leverage Both Content and Skill

Sam Wineburg writes in "Historical Thinking and Other Unnatural Acts" that every encounter with the past produces a moment of tension within the learner: what came before is simultaneously rendered foreign and familiar.[7]

In response to critics who argued that "garden-variety thinking" is the same as historical thinking,[8] he asked high school students, primary school teachers, and history doctoral students to analyze the following article and share what could be key points to discern when thinking critically about it. Try it yourself.

Content Versus Skill Debate—A History Example

Evaluate/analyze the following document:

Source: Proclamation issued by President Harrison, Washington, July 21, 1892. *New York Times*, July 22, 1892, p. 8.

I, Benjamin Harrison, President of the United States of America, do hereby appoint Friday, October 21, 1892, the four hundredth anniversary of the discovery of America by Columbus, as a general holiday for the people of the United States. On that day let the people so far as possible cease from toil and devote themselves to such exercises as may best express honor to the discoverer and their appreciation of the great achievements of the four completed centuries of American life.

Columbus stood in his age as the pioneer of progress and enlightenment. The system of universal education is in our age the most prominent and salutary feature of the spirit of enlightenment, and it is peculiarly appropriate that the schools be made by the people the center of the day's demonstration.

Let the national flag float over every school house in the country, and the exercises be such as shall impress upon our youth the patriotic duties of American citizenship.

In the churches and in the other places of assembly of the people, let there be expressions of gratitude to Divine Providence for the devout faith of the discoverer, and for the Divine care and guidance which has directed our history and so abundantly blessed our people.

Stop & Jot

Evaluate/analyze Harrison's 1892 Proclamation:

_____

_____

_____

After reading Wineburg's article, we replicated this activity with over 200 middle school and high school history teachers as well as middle school and high school instructional leaders. When given this task with no additional context or explanation, they came up with answers like the following:

- "Harrison is trying to establish and strengthen White European culture and Christian values with a holiday that will inculcate youth in these lessons."

- "Harrison wants to unite the country around a White/European hero, insisting on the 'discovery' of America without mention of Indigenous history."

These answers were similar to the ones Wineburg received in his own research.

Look at what happens, however, when we give those same teachers and leaders additional historical information.

History Example, Take 2—Adding Knowledge

Read the following historical information about the end of the 19th century.

End of the 19th Century—Period of Change[9]

- The United States was in a rapid state of change as the 19th century drew to a close.
  - Between 1880 and 1910, 18 million new immigrants came to the United States.
  - This created a population boom.

- This new wave of immigrants, primarily from Southern and Eastern Europe, were different from previous immigrant groups.
  - They looked differently than previous immigrants and spoke different languages.
  - They worshipped differently as well. They tended to be Catholic rather than Protestant.

- As an example, consider Italian Americans:
  - In the early 1880s, there were approximately 300,000 Italians in the United States.
  - That number doubled by 1890.
  - By 1910, there were 2 million Italians in the United States—making up 10% of all immigrants.
  - They practiced Catholicism and settled in cities, along with Poles and Portuguese—forming a new block of immigrants—"the urban Catholic."
  - This was in opposition to the goal of many politicians to create a "melting pot."

- This new group of immigrants presented new challenges.
  - There was a growing sense of nativism as they assimilated slower than previous groups of immigrants and were more easily identified as "other."

- Politicians were working to gain support from these new groups in the population.

Stop & Jot

Re-evaluate/analyze Harrison's 1892 Proclamation using this additional contextual information:

_____
_____
_____

If your experience was anything like ours, you probably have a very different answer (unless you're already skilled in the art of historical thinking yourself!). Wineburg highlighted the different conclusions that came from his own doctoral students:

- The expansion of heroic pantheon to include former undesirables.

- The shameless appeal to superheroes in order to gain votes in urban centers.

- The beginning of Pan-Whiteness in postbellum America; or, the Mediterranean horde gets into the country club.[10]

Where many readers first assume that instituting Columbus Day is about celebrating White European culture, with additional knowledge they realize that in that era Harrison was actually selecting someone who at the time would be considered a "non-white" hero: an Italian. Ironically, he was doing the opposite of what most people now associate with Columbus Day.

There are so many conclusions that you can draw from this activity. For one, we need knowledge of yesterday to evaluate as a historian. Analysis without historical knowledge is not only superficial but inaccurate.

Core Idea

We need knowledge of yesterday, not today, to unlock a source's meaning. Analysis without historical knowledge is not only superficial but inaccurate.

For decades educators have debated about the amount of knowledge needed versus skill. On the one hand, there is E. D. Hirsch and the idea of core knowledge that is fundamental to advance your understanding.[11] On the other hand, you have those who champion critical thinking and the skills needed to solve the complex problems in our society, like Diane Halpern and Robert Ennis.[12] The Harrison declaration analysis bring to light what might feel obvious: you need both content and skill to achieve mastery.

As cognitive scientist Daniel Willingham states:

> Data from the last thirty years lead to a conclusion that is not scientifically challengeable: thinking well requires knowing facts, and that's not true simply because you need something to think *about*. The very processes that teachers care about most—critical thinking processes

such as reasoning and problem solving—are intimately entwined with factual knowledge that is stored in long-term memory (not just found in the environment).[13]

The implications of this exercise are significant. We need to think of teaching as building both content and skill.

This is precisely what Jah'Nique has done by selecting sources that build knowledge, and then teaching historical thinking via four-corner annotations. Armed with knowledge and skills, students can become real historians.

The ability to think historically challenges us to note and confront our own biases, including a view of the past colored by a 21st-century experience. Had we been there, we tell ourselves, we would have surely done things differently! Or how could they not have seen what we do now, or known what was to come? Yet how we understand the past shifts when we make an effort to name the unique circumstances and conditions of historical actors. Behaviors and choices that may have seemed strange and inexplicable suddenly become more understandable, familiar, and human. That is not to say that every decision by every historical actor can or should be justified or explained away by a unique historical context. Historical thinking does not absolve the past. Yet what it can do is build a bridge between yesterday and today. And between those two points, historical empathy can grow.

Core Idea

Historical empathy grows by bridging the gap between today and yesterday.

When done well, students note the underlying connections between themselves and those in the past, while acknowledging the clear differences that influenced the choices these historic actors made and how particular events unfolded. Why does this matter in History class? Fostering historical empathy enables students to approach the past with greater discernment, deepening their potential understanding and analysis. Outside of the classroom, historical empathy provides an additional pathway to create empathy for those around us, which is a critical component in creating future global citizens. When students take on the disciplinary work of considering the unique context with which the historical actors lived, they also start to reconsider the views of those who may not live in the same part of the world as them, or have the same identity markers, and perhaps they will approach these unique views and people with similar empathy.

Put It All Together—Know-Show

Jah'Nique has now done the cognitive work of selecting her sources and unpacking them to prepare to guide students in their development of both knowledge and skill. As a final step, she puts it all together to prepare for her lesson.

Create a Know-Show Chart

Here's how Jah'Nique organized a break-down of all her prep work. What do you notice?

Know-Show Chart

Know-Show	
Know	**Show**
Schema/Background Knowledge	**Historical Thinking**
Themes	• Explain how a historical development or process is related to another historical development or process.
• Locke's ideas of natural rights	**Unpack the Source—Annotations**
• Social contract	• Four corners:
• Mercantilism (view of colonies as serving mother country)	◦ Historical context
• Since European colonization, Latin America had continued to be a vastly unequal place, where the white minority controlled the vast majority of land and resources, while the majority people of color often endured poverty, labor exploitation, and a lack of political rights.	◦ Point of view
	◦ Audience
	◦ Purpose
	• Underline key portions that illuminate the author's claim.
Revolutions	• Significance statement makes note of similarity or difference between the two revolutions.
• Haitian Revolution → inspired movement, but also solidified creole fears of popular uprising → maintain social hierarchy	**Writing**
• Napoleonic Wars: deposed Spanish monarch which delegitimized authority, provided opportunity for independence movement	• Use ANEZ to structure their response to the question:
	◦ A—state argument
	◦ N—name relevant details (key terms)
	◦ E—explain how and why
• Chattel slavery, encomienda system, casta system, whites are minority	◦ Z—zoom out to connect argument to prompt

Know-Show	
Know	**Show**
Key Dates	
• 1775–1784: American Revolution	
• 1789–1799: French Revolution	
• 1791–1804: Haitian Revolution	
• 1803–1815: Napoleonic Wars	
• 1808–1833: Spanish-American wars of Independence	
Vocabulary	
• Simón Bolívar (creole revolutionary who led multiple revolutions in Latin America)	
• Juan Pablo Viscardo (Peruvian creole, wrote "An Open Letter to America")	
• Casta system	
• Caudillo	
• Creole	
• Constitution of Cadiz (radically new Spanish constitution built on Enlightenment ideas that tried to give more power to colonies but still maintain one empire)	

In the creation of this chart, Jah'Nique is asking herself a simple but significant question: What do students need to know and be able to do to answer this prompt?

Core Idea

Teaching starts with a simple question: What do students need to know and be able to do to master this task?

This question bridges the content/skill divide by asking us to address both—what did we need to answer the prompt? Another way to ask this question is, what information and skills are essential, without which students will not be able to answer this prompt to the same depth as I did?

This is not as easy as it sounds, because once we learn something (a piece of knowledge or a skill) we often use it unconsciously in future endeavors. Yet unpacking that assumed knowledge and skill transforms the quality of your teaching.

Jah'Nique uses the structure of a know-show chart to organize this work into essential, discrete areas. The know-show chart makes visible the thinking that allows for argumentation. In a history class, that involves the following:

- Know (Knowledge):
  - Key themes (Enlightenment, natural rights, colonization, revolution)
  - Key dates (dates you need to know to make sense of the order of events surrounding this historical period)
  - Key vocabulary (historical figures, terms, concepts, etc.)

- Show/Do (Skill):
  - Key historical thinking skills
  - Unpacking sources
  - Writing a comprehensive response (thesis, evidence, argumentation, etc.)

By putting all this in one chart, Jah'Nique has equipped herself to analyze her own lesson to see if it provides students the necessary knowledge and skills they need to do historical thinking.

While these sources provide Jah'Nique with vital evidence, so does the outside evidence she's gathered as she built her historical context of the era.

Prepare for Class—Organize the Evidence

In one final step, Jah'Nique creates a chart of the key evidence that she'll be looking for students to produce in class discussion and in their writing. She adds evidence from the sources as well as outside evidence (OE), the additional schema students need to give these sources greater context. Depending on the prompt, she might create a t-chart, Venn diagram, or any organizational structure that helps. Here is a sample from this lesson.

Key Evidence Chart from Sources and Outside Evidence
Latin American Revolutions

Caused by Enlightenment	Other Causes
Enlightenment influence	**Creole desire to preserve—and enhance—their power**
• Property rights—"Spanish commercial monopoly system . . . limitations on what we can legally produce" (Viscardo D1).	• Viscardo sums up creole elite position that mercantilist policies are stifling trade and profit in colonies (D1).
• Political representation—"administration of our own affairs" (Viscardo D1).	• "Disputing the natives for titles of ownership" (Bolívar D2).
• Lack of "freedom" and desire for self-rule (Bolívar D2).	• "We derive our rights from Europe and we have to assert these rights against rights of native" (Bolívar D3).
• OE: Locke's ideas of natural rights, social contract, mercantilism (view of colonies as serving mother country).	• Creoles wanted to prevent popular rebellion and protect property (slaves, etc.) (Bethell D4).
Revolutionary developments in the Atlantic world (arguable for either bucket)	• OE: chattel slavery, encomienda system, casta system, whites are minority.
• OE: Haitian Revolution → inspired movement, but also solidified creole fears of popular uprising → maintain social hierarchy.	
• OE: Napoleonic Wars deposed Spanish monarch which delegitimized authority, provided opportunity for independence movement.	
• OE: American Revolution inspired independence.	

Graphic organizers are a staple feature of Jah'Nique's classroom. They enrich her instruction, helping students keep track of and build ideas before shaping them into arguments

Armed with this framework, Jah'Nique is ready for the next step—building the historical world in which students will immerse themselves.

CONCLUSION

A curious thing happens when we plan backwards from the destination: the journey becomes more exciting. Planning to guide sensemaking for students brings the beautiful realization that so many light bulbs will go off in each stage of the process—building up additional knowledge, acquiring or solidify thinking skills, and coming to a fresh conclusion. All of that is illuminated by the opening prompt and exemplar: the roadmap to guide students on the journey.

With this roadmap in hand the next logical question is, how do we embark on the journey? Or, how do we teach to get there? The next parts of our text will address that directly:

- How we build knowledge when students don't have it
- How we help them grapple with the sources
- How we facilitate discourse to help them make sense of it

Keep reading!

KEY TAKEAWAYS

- Don't recite history; make it.
- The past doesn't change. How we understand it does.
- When we can make sense of the past, we can make history in the present.
- Instruction is rudderless without a destination.
- A proper destination doesn't dictate what you should believe, only what you should be thinking about.
- You eliminate the echo chamber by actively seeking the counterargument.
- Make your lesson engaging by giving your prompt multidirectional purpose.
- The quality of your class prompt will only be as good as the quality of the evidence you have to address it.
- The exemplar response is the starting point for instruction, not the end. It determines the bar for rigor.
- High expectations are set not by what we say, but what we expect—and what we accept—in student writing.
- Select a set of sources that enable students to talk to—and spar with—each other.

- "Source" the document: contextualize its content to unpack its meaning.
- Name the corners to frame the meaning.
- We need knowledge of yesterday, not today, to unlock a source's meaning. Analysis without historical knowledge is not only superficial but inaccurate.
- Historical empathy grows by bridging the gap between today and yesterday.
- Teaching starts with a simple question: What do my students need to know and be able to do to master this task?

Planning Template—Intellectual Preparation for Instruction

TEXT(s): Name of the text/document(s) or topic for the discourse:
CLASS PROMPT: Main inquiry question that students will answer after the discourse—think 4QM: (SHEG calls this the Central Historical Question.)
Your final writing prompt:
EXEMPLAR RESPONSES: Craft plausible, historically defensible responses to the prompt that take different angles.
Response 1: Response 2:
PROMPTS FOR DISCOURSE: Questions and prompts to guide student discourse:
(NOTE: More guidance to be given in Part 4 for this section.)
BUILD KNOWLEDGE—Plan for student readiness: Building a baseline so all students can engage successfully in the discourse:
(NOTE: More guidance will be given in Part 2 for this section.)

SELF-ASSESSMENT

Part 1: Define the Destination	Score
Choose the Sources • Offer multiple perspectives of a historical actor, event, or development (e.g., dominant and overlooked voices, left- and right-leaning, etc.). • Manageable for the time that you have (one-page source per class period or four-paragraph-long sources).	__/ 10
Design the Prompt and Exemplar Responses • Prompt is clear and specific (4QM), compelling (relevant and thought-provoking), multifaceted (multiple possible answers), and manageable (doable in the time allotted). • Prompt addresses a key historical thinking skill. • Exemplar responses set the bar for what students should do to meet the task's demand. • Know-show chart names the knowledge and skills students need for the task.	__/ 10
Part 1 Score:	____/20

PLANNING FOR ACTION

- Which key ideas from this section resonate the most for you?

- How will you take and/or modify these resources to meet the needs of your class(es)?

_____

_____

_____

Action	Date

Build Knowledge

"Every addition to true knowledge is an addition to human power."
—Horace Mann

"The end of all knowledge should surely be service to others."
—Cesar Chavez

The end of the 15th century has long been viewed by many historians as a seminal moment in world history. Many narratives of that time period note Christopher Columbus's journeys from Europe to the Americas beginning in 1492, which launched a long period of European colonization of the continent. They also note Vasco de Gama's travels, which established trade routes to India and expanded European cultural influence worldwide. Indeed, until the last few decades the dominant historiographical narrative, and therefore the general public's understanding, was that Europe rose to power after 1492 because of its superior military technology, governmental organization, and its capitalist spirit of competition.

That narrative has been complicated by the arguments of several contemporary historians, including prominent voices like Jared Diamond, J.R. McNeill, and Lydia Shaffer, who propose conflicting understandings of the rise of the West. Diamond bases his argument largely on geography,[1] which McNeill critiques as geographical determinism.[2] Shaffer, in turn, seeks to undermine the dominant narrative that the non-Western world has been emulating the West in its technology and sciences. She turns the argument on its head, claiming that the West was in fact emulating the "South."[3] Shaffer explores the ways in which the rise of the West was not only contingent upon, but also in many ways sought to emulate, developments that originated in Southern Asia, from the cultivation of cotton and sugar to navigational technology. Labeling this phenomenon Southernization, she puts this in direct tension with Westernization.

Into this powerful academic debate wades Rachel Blake, teacher of 10th-grade World History. In her next unit, her students will examine the factors behind the rise of the West in the 15th century. How can she make this history come alive for her students, who at this point have very little context and knowledge about the time period? How can she bring them into this academic debate and guide them to come to their own conclusions?

Let's enter her classroom and find out.

Class Launch

Lesson: Interrogating the "Rise of the West"

Papers rustle as students flip through the course reader. Rachel quickly scans the room to make sure everyone has a notebook out and open and that the course reader is open to the Knowledge Organizer. They do. She's ready to begin.

RACHEL (TEACHER):	Who recognizes the date 1492? Can you tell me something about it?
TALIA:	Of course. That's when Christopher Columbus sailed to America.
RACHEL (TEACHER):	Precisely. What can you recall about what happened as a result of his voyages?
BELLA:	We saw the colonization of the Americas by a bunch of countries like England. I remember in middle school we debated whether Columbus was a hero or a villain.
RACHEL (TEACHER):	That's a strong start. Let me ask you another question. Take a look at the board [shows the image on the following page]. What do you know about Westernization? What does it mean to you? Turn and talk.

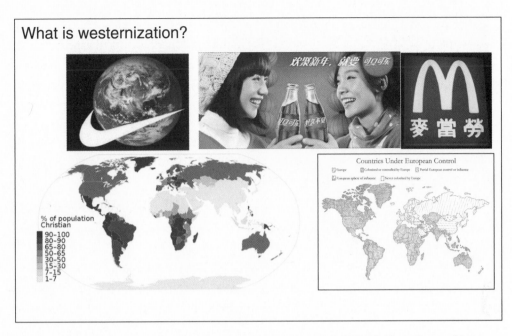

What is westernization?

% of population
Christian
90-100
80-90
65-80
50-65
30-50
15-30
7-15
1-7

Countries Under European Control

Source (a): NASA/Public domain; (b): Starcom Worldwide, Inc.; (c): McDonald; (d): outline-world-map.

After a short turn and talk, students share out anecdotes of Westernization in music, culture, and colonization in various parts of the world.

RACHEL (TEACHER): Fascinating. So we have a lot of ideas associated with this term. Today, we are going to build on that knowledge and go deeper. You see, historians have often labeled this period as "The Rise of the West": when Europe starts to expand its power and influence, not only in America but across the globe. These historians might argue that this Rise of the West is exemplified by Columbus's voyage and the subsequent European colonization of the Americas.

But something fascinating has happened in just the past 20 years. Historians have gotten into a massive debate: Should we consider the end of the 15th century as the rise of the West and beginning of global westernization? Or should we see it differently? I'm not going to decide this answer: you are. But first you need to meet the historians on all sides of this debate. And you need a bit of knowledge to make your assessment.

Please take a look at the Knowledge Organizer in your Course Reader. I want to draw your attention to two terms that we will encounter today . . .

Over the rest of the class period, Rachel begins to immerse students into what will feel for many to be a strange, new world. At first glance, there is nothing special about Rachel's instruction. But look a little closer. Rachel takes the ordinary and makes it extraordinary by building up their knowledge.

> ### Core Idea
> Take the ordinary and make it extraordinary by building up their knowledge.

At the heart of great History instruction is something that is compelling: a reason to learn. What is striking is that you won't find the lesson compelling if you don't have knowledge of its nuance.

As we introduced in Part 1, building knowledge is essential for students to be able to do genuine historical thinking and analysis—and also to be compelled to do so. So how does Rachel build knowledge? By supercharging two practices that are as old as time:

- Activate knowledge (what students already know).
- Frontload knowledge (what students need).

In the following section, we'll examine each one in depth.

ACTIVATE KNOWLEDGE

If you look back at the opening vignette of Rachel's class, you'll note that the first step she takes in launching her lesson is asking students what they know about 1492, and later about Westernization. This is more than just an engagement strategy: Rachel is activating knowledge—a key cognitive skill.

What we already know has a powerful impact on what we're able to learn, yet much of the energy when we teach is focused on introducing new content and skills. Therein lies the challenge. The human brain stores new information in working memory (formerly known as short-term memory). This storage area has a limited capacity—information that goes there is quickly forgotten. How quickly? In the 1880s, psychologist Hermann Ebbinghaus ran a series of experiments to quantify the rate at which people forget information when it is not reinforced by or connected to prior knowledge. After an hour, participants forgot more than 50% of what they had learned. By the next day they'd lost 66% and by the sixth day, 75%.[4] Statistics like that don't bode well for the demands of the average History class.

But there's a way around our natural forgetfulness. Consider this thought exercise. Recall the street address of your local post office. Unless you visit this location on a regular basis, this task will likely take some time. Now try to recall one of your childhood street addresses. For many of us, a street name and number immediately spring to mind. What makes the biggest difference between what we forget and what we remember? Knowledge retrieval.

Core Idea

The difference between what we forget and what we remember is knowledge retrieval.

This childhood address still exists in your memory because it's meaningful to you, and you've recalled it countless times since the moment you first learned it. To engrave the address of the post office as thoroughly, you'd have to retrieve it, again and again, from your working memory. Regular recall eventually transfers this address to a different, more permanent location: long-term memory. Retrieval solidifies what we know to make it last.

So how do we make prior knowledge more readily available to students? In *Powerful Teaching*, cognitive scientist Pooja Agarwal and social studies teacher Patricia Bain cite retrieval practice as the underutilized key to unlock student learning. Agarwal and fellow scientists note that "struggling to learn—through the act of 'practicing' what you know and recalling information—is much more effective than re-reading, taking notes, or listening to lectures. Slower, effortful retrieval leads to long-term learning. In contrast, fast, easy strategies only lead to short-term learning."[5] Strategies shared in *Powerful Teaching* and Agarwal's website Retrieval Practice (https://www.retrievalpractice.org/) all support the transfer of information from short- to long-term memory. These include spacing (revisiting content over time), interleaving (having students differentiate between closely related concepts), and feedback-driven metacognition (having students think about retrieval).[6]

Knowledge activation through consistent retrieval practice has yet another important benefit in History classrooms. In *Culturally Responsive Teaching and the Brain*, educator Zaretta Hammond shares recent cognitive research that suggests that the brain releases oxytocin, a bonding hormone, in the presence of positive, trusting connection.[7] A simple teacher move like validating successful knowledge retrieval becomes a double-booster for learning: not only does it build trust and rapport with students, it also strengthens and solidifies knowledge.

Once prior knowledge is activated, it becomes available for myriad purposes. In History class, students can use it to link to or contextualize new knowledge, fuel analysis, craft arguments or propose new ideas.

> ## Core Idea
>
> Activating knowledge activates the brain: you make connections between what you already know and what you're about to learn.

What follows are a few simple ways that teachers like Rachel use to activate knowledge as part of their daily routines.

Do Nows

The first 15 minutes of class are an ideal time to activate knowledge. What follows is the "Do Now"—a quick activity to launch a class period, often writing based, that students completed before the opening vignette. What impact does Rachel's Do Now activity have on students? (See the Do Now in its entirety on the following page. As additional context, students have already finished a unit on the Americas before European arrival and read an excerpt of Diamond's *Guns, Germs, and Steel*.)

This Do Now is brief but effective. In less than 10 minutes, students are asked to recall previously taught content—the outcome of Pizarro's encounter with the Incas and Diamond's argument about the role of geography in the rise of Europe. This is an example of what Agarwal and Bain call *spacing*, or revisiting content after an interval of forgetting, which encourages the creation of long-term memories.[8] By reviewing notes or the reading itself to answer these questions, students can ground themselves in the historical narratives that will be challenged later in the lesson. With this simple activity, Rachel can also check in on every student to stamp the key understandings and correct misconceptions or poor retrieval, which establishes a ground floor of knowledge for all of her students at the start of the lesson. Right from the beginning, she is ensuring that no students are left out of the thinking and doing of her lesson.

Rachel's Do Now

Name: _____   Period: _____   Date: _____

Lesson 1.1 – **Interrogating "The Rise of the West"**: *Guns, Germs & Steel*

OBJECTIVE :

SWBAT identify the immediate and long-term factors that facilitated European conquest of the Americas in the Early Modern Era, according to Jared Diamond

QUESTION :

According to Jared Diamond, how did Eurasian geography provide an advantage to the Spanish in their conquest of the Aztec and Inca Empires?

Image courtesy of Vecteezy

DO NOW:

1. Which of the following summarizes a theory that historians have put forward in past generations to explain Europe's rise to power in the Early Modern Era?

    a. Unlike those living in warmer climates, Europeans had the benefit of cold winters which served as the catalyst for ingenuity and invention.
    b. Europeans were more violent than those they conquered in Asia, Africa and the Americas.
    c. God favored the Europeans because he wanted them to spread Christianity around the world.
    d. Europeans were more intelligent than the people of other regions.
    e. All of the above.

2. What was the outcome of Francisco Pizarro's encounter with the Incan ruler, Atahualpa?

    a. Atahualpa's army was much larger than Pizarro's which helped them defeat the Spanish.
    b. Pizarro's men, despite being vastly outnumbered, were able to defeat the Inca.
    c. The Incan people converted to Christianity after encountering the Spanish conquistador and his army.
    d. Most of Pizarro's men succumbed to diseases before reaching Atahualpa.

3. What were the "immediate reasons" that Diamond provides to explain why the Europeans were able to conquer native peoples in the Americas? (See p. 5)

    •

    •

    •

    •

    •

    •

Additional Do Now Activities for Retrieval

Rachel varies her Do Now activities to strengthen and reinforce long-term knowledge retention. A short list of Do Now activities from this unit follows. Cognitive research shows these are particularly effective retrieval strategies.[9]

Sample Do Now—Contrast Prior Knowledge with Other, Closely Related Terms (Interleaving)

<u>DO NOW</u>: Re-write each term below its place of origin (i.e. silk → China).

Image adapted from the AP World History Curriculum Framework (College Board)

WESTERN EUROPE	INDIA	SOUTHEAST ASIA	CHINA

"Arabic" numerals	caravel	porcelain
Champa rice	cotton	printing
compass	gunpowder	spices
concept of zero	mercantilism	sugar

Sample Do Now—Apply It to Relevant Contexts

"And when we saw so many cities and villages built in the water and other great towns on dry land and that straight and level causeway going toward [Tenochtitlan], we were amazed... on account of the great towers and [temples] and buildings rising from the water, and all built of masonry. And some of our soldiers even asked whether the things that we saw were not a dream? It is not to be wondered at that I here write it down in this manner, for there is so much to think over that I do not know how to describe it, seeing things as we did that had never been heard of or seen before, not even dreamed about."

Bernal Diaz del Castillo, Spanish soldier, personal account of encountering Aztec capital city, Tenochtitlan, in the late 15th century

1. Based on Castillo's account, which of the following can be most clearly inferred about Aztec society in the 15th century?
   a. The Aztec Empire was a highly centralized state which allowed for the construction of monumental architecture and agricultural innovations.
   b. The Aztec Empire had established a state-religion, and mandated that their subjects practiced this religion.
   c. The Aztec military forces were more advanced in their weaponry and techniques than the Spanish conquistadores.
   d. The Aztecs engaged in long-distance trade with the Inca Empire in South America.

2. The Spanish soldiers' view of the Aztec capital city is best understood in the context of which of the following?
   a. The establishment of a direct maritime route from Europe to the markets of Asia
   b. The first encounter of Europeans with a native American society
   c. The decline in mean global temperatures which impacted both agricultural and migration patterns
   d. Growing connections between the Eastern and Western Hemispheres made possible by advancements in transoceanic voyaging

3. In what modern-day country did the account above take place?
   a. Dominican Republic
   b. The Philippines
   c. Mexico
   d. Peru

4. Which of the following statements makes an accurate comparison of the Aztec and Inca empires prior to Spanish conquest?
   a. Both the Aztec and Inca used terrace farms to adapt to their environments.
   b. While the Incan Empire maintained a highly stratified social structure, Aztec society was characterized by a high degree of social mobility.
   c. While the Aztec engaged in long-distance trade, the Inca remained isolated by the Andes Mountains.
   d. Both the Aztec and Inca relied on a tribute system to provide them with desirable items ranging from taxes to labor.

Sample Do Now—Evaluate Its Significance

2. At the time of the Spaniards' arrival in the New World, Aztec society was
   a. Greatly fragmented due to mounting tensions between the nobles and the ruler
   b. Primarily agricultural with small farming villages scattered throughtout the region
   c. Highly centralized and militaristic with complex cities throughtout its territory
   d. Ethinically diverse due to the arrival of Quechua-speaking Inca in their territory

3. Which of the following statements makes an accurate comparison of the Aztec and Inca empires prior to Spanish conquest?
   a. Both the Aztec and Inca used terrace farms to their environments.
   b. Both the Aztec and Inca relied on a tribute system to provide them with desirable items ranging from taxes to labor.
   c. While the Incan Empire maintained a highly stratified social structure, Aztec society was characterized by a high degree of social mobility.
   d. While the Aztec engaged in long-distance trade, the Inca remained isolated by the Andes Mountains.

4. Evaluate the factors, according to Jared Diamond, that facilitated the European colorization of the Americas? Which factor do you think was most significant? Explain why.

Sample Do Now—Create a Network of Connections to the Learned Term (Concept Mapping)

> **OBJECTIVE :**
> SWBAT analyze how J.R. McNeill builds his argument in "The World According to Jared Diamond"

DO NOW: Based on the arguments of McNeill and Diamond, in the space below, create a concept map showing the immediate and long-term factors that allowed the Spanish to conquer the Aztec and Inca empires.

IMMEDIATE	LONG-TERM
1. **Superior weaponry** (rifles and cannons vs swords)	1. **Geographic luck** – Europe was part of Eurasia, which had MANY usable domesticated animals (horse, pig, cow, sheep, goat) while the Americas had only 1 large animal that humans could tame and put to work (alpaca/llama)
2. **Horses** (mounted cavalry = terrifying & effective weapon → military advantage, despite being outnumbered)	2. **Agriculture → civilization**
3. **Ships & navigations methods**	3. **Agriculture (and other technology) spread from its origin in Fertile Crescent along East -West axis for 2 reasons:**
4. **Writing system** that allowed for rapid communication	- These plants and animals could thrive best in fairly narrow E-W latitude band
5. **Highly centralized political organization** that allowed governments to fund expeditions	- Fertile Crescent is part of Eurasia oriented E-W, different than Americas, Africa
6. **Infectious disease** which decimated the native populations, weakening their resistance capacity.	4. **Domesticated animals led to immunity** → ability to live near animals and infected people without getting sick
NOT: Europeans were more intelligent, cold winters in Europe spurred ingenuity & invention, others were more peace-loving and Europeans were violent, God favored Christian Europe	

Do Nows aren't the only way to support knowledge retrieval in the classroom. Quick class oral review can also achieve the same end. Let's take a look.

Class Oral Review

A class oral review can be leveraged as a way to review and retrieve large swaths of knowledge that students will need to move forward. Watch this clip from Dan Balmert's 10th-grade AP World History classroom. They have just finished their unit on World War I and are starting to study the time period after World War I, particularly the introduction of communism in Russia and China. What does Dan say and do to launch his class?

WATCH Clip 1: Dan Balmert—Class Oral Review

This transcription comes from the first minute of the class oral review. Watch the full clip to see how much content Dan is able to review in just 3½ minutes.

Class Oral Review—Content

DAN (TEACHER):	Topics for review for today are WWI's causes and impacts, the Russian Revolution, the Cold War, and Chinese Communism. Turn and talk.

[Students review notes on the selected topics and talk in pairs until Dan cues the class to come together. Students stand behind chairs].

DAN (TEACHER):	Jumping all the way back to the beginning of the unit, WWI is sparked by which major event? [Pauses, looks around the room.] Sydney.
SYDNEY:	It was sparked by the assassination of Austro-Hungarian Archduke Ferdinand.
DAN:	Good. There are four main causes, the long-term causes. We had an acronym. What are the four main causes of WW1? [Pauses.] Christian.
CHRISTIAN:	Militarism, alliances, industrialism—
DAN:	Close, but no.
CHRISTIAN [SELF-CORRECTS]:	imperialism and nationalism.

Dan knows a thing or two about working with young people. Making this activity kinesthetic (asking students to stand) shakes out some of the stupor of being seated all day and creates a bright line between the start of class and the upcoming instruction. Over the course of a few minutes, he randomly calls on students to answer questions, making everyone feel part of the class (what you cannot see in the clip is that Dan also provides pre-calls for students who require extra think time before the start of the class oral review). Students also have the opportunity to work in pairs to review their notes and knowledge organizers and to contextualize the upcoming prompt.

Think about the power of these activities. On the foundation of a classroom culture of trust and rapport, Dan has built a culture that allows students to leverage him and each other to be prepared to be successful. Class oral reviews are not "gotchas." If a student answered incorrectly, as Christian does for part of his response, Dan could use a variety of techniques, like pre-calling, asking a follow-up question, or calling on another student and then looping back to the original student to provide the answer. The outcome of Dan's class oral review activity is that everyone recalls and hears accurate information repeatedly so as to begin to embed that knowledge into their long-term memory.

> ### Core Idea
>
> Class oral review embeds knowledge into long-term memory.

As cognitive scientist Daniel Willingham notes in *Why Don't Students Like School*, "Practice yields three benefits: (1) it can help the mental process become automatic and thereby enable further learning; (2) it makes memory long lasting; and (3) it increases the likelihood that learning will transfer to new situation."[10]

Class oral reviews can also target a specific disciplinary skill that students have learned in the past. Let's visit Neha Marvania's 6th-grade World History class. They have been studying the Enlightenment-era revolutions in Latin America. As you watch the clip, how does Neha build disciplinary skills to accompany knowledge retrieval?

 WATCH Clip 2: Neha Marvania—Class Oral Review

Class Oral Review—Skill

NEHA (TEACHER): What is the benefit of remembering events in chronological order when it comes to history? Take 30 seconds.

[Students talk in pairs while Neha circulates. At the end of 30 seconds, Neha calls the class together and asks one student to share out.]

NATASHA: The importance of remembering them [events] in order because we need to know what event happened first, and how it affected later events. For example, since John Locke developed the Theory of Natural Rights, it inspired people to get more ideas about government and make a democracy, not a monarchy.

NEHA (TEACHER): Excellent. In a moment, we are going to play a timeline game. Take the blue index cards* that are in front of you. You are going to put them in chronological order, and then talk through why one event led to the next. Work with your partner. You have 1 minute. Go!

[*Each index card had one of the following Enlightenment-era events: The Haitian Revolution, Latin American revolutions, Spanish-American wars of independence, and John Locke's Theory of Natural Rights.]

Neha's timeline activity is more than just a fun and engaging activity for students. When a disciplinary skill like chronological reasoning is locked in, students have a significant advantage: they can evaluate their understanding of the time period more easily. Was Toussaint Louverture really inspired by John Locke and his Theory of Natural Rights, or was there something else driving Louverture and the Haitian Revolution? These are the powerful questions that historians spend their time examining. By activating prior knowledge, students ready themselves to do the same.

Do Nows and Class Oral Reviews help students activate knowledge right before learning new content. Teachers like Rachel, Neha, and Dan vary these opening activities to provide students with different ways to demonstrate knowledge (orally versus written) as well multiple ways to work (singly, in pairs, in groups). These decisions enable them to reach all the different types of students in the classroom, creating a more inclusive, equitable classroom.

While knowledge retrieval is a superb way to start off the lesson, it is also valuable throughout the lesson.

Supply (or Create) a Resource

At the start of each unit, Rachel gives her students what she calls a Knowledge Organizer. Take a look.

Knowledge Organizer Sample 1—Rise of the West

Note: The full one-pager contains 41 terms. This excerpted portion has been expanded to make the writing more legible.

APWH Reference Sheet 1.1
Unit 1 – Interrogating the "Rise of the West"

		Key Terms
Navigational Technology *adapted from Asian, Islamic and Classical civilizations*		
1.	**astrolabe**	origins in Classical Greece, this tool allows navigators to use the sun to measure the latitude of their ship at sea
2.	astronomical charts	star map – by developing better maps of the night sky, Europeans were able to better navigate using constellations as guides
3.	cartography	map-making – through the sponsorship of Ptg. Prince Henry the Navigator, Ptg. (then more broadly European) knowledge of map-making and geography ↑
4.	**compass**	crucial navigational tool that originated in China, uses magnetism to tell the cardinal direction the user is facing (North-East-South-West)
5.	**lateen triangular sails**	common feature of Euro ships (origin S. Asian dhow ship), effective b/c allows sailors to tack "against the wind" → easier to sail regardless of wind direction
6.	Prince Henry the Navigator	Portuguese initiator of "Age of Discovery" thru sponsorship of innovations in navigational tech, exploration W. coast of Africa (searching for gold + Prester John)
7.	volta do mar	in Ptg. "turn of the sea," navigational technique perfected by Ptg. sailors allowing them to understand trade winds and currents (like I.O. monsoon winds)
European Innovations in ship design		
8.	**caravel**	small, highly maneuverable sailing ship developed by Portuguese in 15th c.to explore W. Africa coast (ex. La Niña used on Columbus's journey to the Americas)
9.	carrack	replaced the caravel, this is a 3 or 4-mast ship, larger cargo area allowed for greater profit and longer voyages; replaced in 17th c. by larger Spanish **galleons**
10.	fluyt	17th c. Dutch sailing vessel designed for efficient transoceanic voyages; had ample cargo space, only needed small crew; ↓ Dutch cost of transportation (VOC)
Motives		
11.	**Christopher Columbus**	Italian explorer sent by Spanish monarchs Ferdinand & Isabel to find maritime route to Asia → landed in Caribbean → initiated European colonization of Ams.
12.	commodity	a raw material or agricultural product that can be bought and sold (i.e. cotton, tea, coffee, silk, etc.)
13.	**demand**	the amount of consumer desire for a certain commodity (the higher the demand, usually the higher the price that can be charged if the supply is low)
14.	Italian city-states	Venice, Milan, Florence, Genoa etc. were crucial trade links btw. Europe & Asia in Post-Classical→ Early Modern; Venice had monopoly on spice trade via Arabs
15.	**Ottoman conquest of Constantinople**	1453: Islamic gunpowder empire conquered capital of Byzantine (Christian) Emp, turning point prompting ↑ Euro search for maritime route to Asia
16.	**Reconquista**	700-year war fought by Christians in Iberian Peninsula to overthrow Muslim rule (Al-Andalus), ended w/ Chr. victory in 1492 and expulsion of Jews & Muslims
17.	spice trade	cloves, cinnamon, pepper, nutmeg etc. originated SE Asia; high demand in Afro-Eurasia since Classical, traded Silk Rds. & I.O. → motivated Euro. maritime trade

1491: Separate Hemispheres	1492: Columbus & Global Connections	1501: Encomienda (coerced labor) system begins
• In the <u>Western Hemisphere</u> (Americas), major empires include Aztec in modern day Mexico, the Inca in modern day Peru, with 100s of North Am. civilizations like the Cherokee, Iroquois, Mississippians, Pueblos, Navajo, etc. • <u>Eastern Hemisphere</u> (Afro-Eurasia) powerful empires in Asia included Ming & Ottoman; vibrant trade in Indian Ocean, Silk Roads, Trans-Sahara, Mediterranean; pop. increasing after devastation of Bubonic Plague c. 1300	• Reconquista ends in Catholic victory over Spain • Spanish Catholic monarchs Ferdinand & Isabel commission Columbus's voyage to India • Columbus instead landed in the Caribbean • Columbian Exchange begins, a biological transfer between Old and New World • Taíno, Native people of Caribbean, die in large numbers due to introduction of smallpox • Columbus promoted enslavement of natives	• Acc. to feudalism, natives owed tribute to Sp. Crown • The Sp. Crown awarded land grants w/ rights to native American labor 1st to conquistadores, later to Sp. immigrants, called *encomenderos* • *Encomenderos* were responsible for their native laborers' instruction in Spanish language and Catholic faith and to provide them security • Native chiefs were responsible for ensuring labor • Led to harsh abuses of natives and ↑ death rates
1513: Europeans "discover" Pacific Ocean & N. Am.	1519-1521: Spanish conquest of the Aztec Empire	1532-1572: Spanish conquest of the Incan Empire
• Conquistador Vasco Nuñez de Balboa established the 1st European settlement on mainland America in modern-day Panama, in his search for gold, he was 1st European to "discover" the Pacific Ocean • Spanish conquistador, Juan Ponce de Leon, "discovers" Florida, but failed in his attempt to est. a colony b/c of native resistance	• 1519: Cortes' expedition left Cuba for Mexico, expedition aided by La Malinche and native alliances; met, then later captured Moctezuma • Warfare between Spanish & Aztec soldiers • 1521: fall of Tenochtitlan = beginning of Sp. rule in Mexico, where they est. their capital city, Mexico City on ruins of Tenochtitlan • 1535: Viceroyalty of New Spain established	• c. 1528, prior to Spanish arrival in their territory, Inca emperor died from smallpox → a civil war began between his sons • 1532: Battle of Cajamarca, 168 Sp. soldiers led by Pizarro captured Inca leader Atahualpa • Decades of warfare → Tupac Amaru, last Inca emperor captured & executed in Cusco 1572 • 1572: Viceroyalty of Peru established

Spanish Codex shows Aztec tribute

Image Source: (a): El Comandante / Wikimedia Commons / Public Domain

Knowledge Organizer Sample 2—Westernization or Southernization?

APWH Reference Sheet 1.2
Unit 2 – Westernization or Southernization?

		Key Terms
General		
1.	southernization	process of technological innovation that originated in South Asia, which contributed to the rise of China, and ultimately the rise of the West
2.	westernization	process whereby non-Western societies adopt Western culture (i.e. industry, technology, law, culture, lifestyle, education, clothing, language, etc.)
Originated in Southern Asia		
1.	Buddhism	founded N. India, Classical Era by Siddhartha Gautama, based on 4 Noble Truths, 8-Fold Path, achieving Nirvana, spread via trade to E, SE Asia → syncretism
2.	Champa rice	fast-ripening, drought resistant rice developed in Vietnam, introduced to China in Post-Classical → increased food supply → China's overall pop. increased 2x
3.	compass	crucial navigational tool that originated in China, uses magnetism to tell the cardinal direction the user is facing (North-East-South-West)
4.	cotton	1st domesticated Ancient Era Indus River Valley → trade w/ Mesopotamia → overseas export ↑ b/c demand ↑; desirable b/c soft texture & can be dyed any color
5.	gunpowder	Post-Classical Chinese invention, spread westward via Mongol Empire & Silk Roads, adapted and refined by many including Europeans to improve weaponry
6.	knowledge of monsoon winds	before 300 BCE, Malay sailors (from SE Asia) began to ride seasonal monsoon winds to navigate I.O.; Malays also 1st to dev. long-distance spice trade
7.	mathematics	Gupta dynasty: concept of zero developed & "Arabic" numerals (the Europeans b/c introduced to these by Arabs) → allowed for efficient, advanced calculations
8.	paper & printing	developed in Buddhist monasteries between 700-750 C.E., China was one of earliest centers → tech spread westward via Mongols & Arabs
9.	spices	pepper & cinnamon originated in S. Asia, nutmeg & cloves SE Asian islands; in great demand in Mid. E & Europe from Classical Era b/c taste & medicinal uses
10.	sugar	during the Gupta dynasty around 350 CE, Indians discovered how to crystallize sugar → could be easily stored & transported → trade commodity
Continuities in Indian Ocean Trade		
11.	African slave trade	slavery in Africa continued in its traditional forms, including incorporation of slaves into households and the export of slaves to Mediterranean & Indian Ocean
12.	diasporic merchant comm.	as in Post-Classical, Arabs & Persian merchants settled in E. Africa, Chinese merchants in SE Asia, and Malay merchants throughout I.O. → cultural diffusion
13.	I.O. Asian merchants	merchants who were Swahili Arabs, Omanis, Gujaratis, and Javanese (mostly Muslim) continued to play a **dominant** role in facilitating Indian Ocean trade
14.	Intra-Asian trade	trade within Asia via Silk Roads and Indian Ocean remained strong during Early Modern Era, despite European entry into these trade networks
15.	commodities	silk, cotton, spices, porcelain etc. remained in demand in this time, including among Asian consumers, which explains why the goods being exchanged were CTs
16.	navigational technology	as in the Post-Classical Era, compass, astrolabe, lateen sails, knowledge of monsoon winds, etc. continued to facilitate safe & efficient trade in the I.O.
Changes in Indian Ocean Trade		
17.	armed trade	Ptg. ships had onboard cannons, used to devastate coastal fortifications; superior firepower secured Europeans foothold in IO trade → est. fortified bases in IO
18.	cartaz	aim of Ptg. trading post emp. was to control commerce (not territory), so Ptg. tried to require all merchant ships to pay duties/tax of 6-10% on cargo to pass
19.	Dutch spice monopoly	Dutch East India Co. (VOC) est. monopoly-total control of spice trade (cinnamon, cloves) via violence & conquest of SE Asia "Spice Islands"; grew very wealthy
20.	European-specific exports	c. 1600, Asian artisans began producing products (i.e. porcelain, cotton textiles) tailored to suit tastes of Euro consumers showing ↑ trade + mass consumption
21.	isolationist trade policies	China est. "Canton System" to limit European trade to 1 port; Tokugawa Japan closed off country to outside influence—by penalty of death—w/ few exceptions
22.	Jesuits	Society of Jesus est. 1534 by Ignatius of Loyola in Spain; sent missions globally to evangelize, worked to spread Christianity in Latin America, Asia & Africa
23.	joint-stock companies	British & Dutch East India Cos. were private trading companies that received govt. charters... granted power to make war, collect taxes & govern
24.	mercantilism	European economic theory arguing a country should acquire colonies for raw materials & export more goods than importing → increased rivalries & imperialism
25.	Omani rivalry	sultanate of Oman resisted Ptg. role in IO, demonstrates Europeans were met with strong resistance to entry into IO, and often repelled by stronger local states
26.	Seven Years' War	1756-63: global conflict principally btw. Britain & France + allies → result = Br. win (gained Fr. territory in now Canada, Florida, Caribbean) → ↑ Br. world power
27.	Portuguese trade posts	used armed trade to est. fortified bases at key IO locations: Mombasa (E Africa), Hormuz (Persian Gulf entrance), Goa (India), Malacca (SE Asia), Macao (China)
28.	Spanish Philippines	in effort to compete w/ rival Ptg., Sp conquered key islands off coast of China; became strategic trade location linking Europe & Asia especially the silver trade
29.	Vasco da Gama	Portuguese sailor, 1st to link Europe to Asia by an ocean route, arrived in India in search of spices in 1498 → led to est. Ptg. trade posts & ↑ Euro imp. in Asia
Social & Cultural Impacts of ↑ Trade - Europe		
30.	growth of merchant class	increased volume of global trade in Early Modern Era → increased power & wealth of merchants → more funding for mass art & culture
31.	Renaissance	14th – 17th c: artistic & literary golden age in Europe, drew on Classical Greek humanism, was result of ↑ merchant $ from trade w/ Asia in Italian city-states
32.	Scientific Revolution	16th – 18th c: series of theories & discoveries by Euro thinkers (i.e. Copernicus, Galileo) based in observation & experimentation → innovations and ↓ religion
33.	tea	Asian luxury goods eventually became mass consumer goods in Europe b/c Br. monopoly on commodity trade (like tea), which lowered price, making affordable
34.	William Shakespeare	16th/17th c. Br. playwright during golden age of Elizabethan England, reflects ↑ merchants' profits & govt. taxes → ↑ arts funding for mass audiences & ↑ literacy
Social & Cultural Impacts of ↑ Trade - Asia		
35.	intensification of peasant labor	b/c of increased global demand, silk production in China & cotton in India, increased dramatically, often accompanied by abuse & coercion of workers
36.	growth of merchant class	increased volume of global trade → increased power & wealth of merchants, despite lower status in Confucianism; → more funding for mass art & culture
37.	Kabuki theatre	Japanese theatre est. Edo Pd known for stylized drama & elaborate make-up, reflects ↑ merchants' profits & govt. taxes → ↑ arts funding for mass audiences
38.	wood block paintings	Japan adopted Chinese movable type during Edo Pd (Tokugawa) to produce art for mass audiences, most famous ex = "Great Wave of Kanagawa" by Hokusai

APWH Reference Sheet 1.2

Unit 2 – Westernization or Southernization?

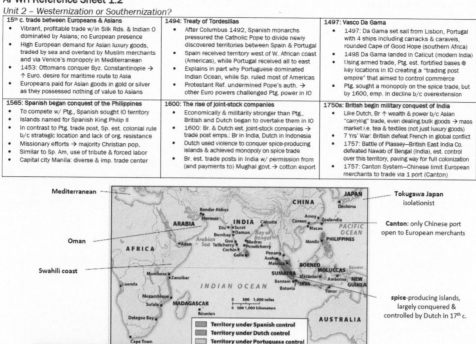

15th c. trade between Europeans & Asians	1494: Treaty of Tordesillas	1497: Vasco Da Gama
• Vibrant, profitable trade w/in Silk Rds. & Indian O dominated by Asians; no European presence • High European demand for Asian luxury goods, traded by sea and overland by Muslim merchants and via Venice's monopoly in Mediterranean • 1453: Ottomans conquer Byz. Constantinople → ↑ Euro. desire for maritime route to Asia • Europeans paid for Asian goods in gold or silver as they possessed nothing of value to Asians	• After Columbus 1492, Spanish monarchs pressured the Catholic Pope to divide newly discovered territories between Spain & Portugal • Spain received territory west of W. African coast (Americas), while Portugal received all to east • Explains in part why Portuguese dominated Indian Ocean, while Sp. ruled most of Americas • Protestant Ref. undermined Pope's auth. → other Euro powers challenged Ptg. power in IO	• 1497: Da Gama set sail from Lisbon, Portugal with 4 ships including carracks & caravels, rounded Cape of Good Hope (southern Africa) • 1498 Da Gama landed in Calicut (modern India) • Using armed trade, Ptg. est. fortified bases @ key locations in IO creating a "trading post empire" that aimed to control commerce • Ptg. sought a monopoly on the spice trade, but by 1600, emp. in decline b/c overextension
1565: Spanish began conquest of the Philippines	1600: The rise of joint-stock companies	1750s: British begin military conquest of India
• To compete w/ Ptg., Spanish sought IO territory • Islands named for Spanish King Philip II • In contrast to Ptg. trade post, Sp. est. colonial rule b/c strategic location and lack of org. resistance • Missionary efforts → majority Christian pop. • Similar to Sp. Am, use of tribute & forced labor • Capital city Manila: diverse & imp. trade center	• Economically & militarily stronger than Ptg., British and Dutch began to overtake them in IO • 1600: Br. & Dutch est. joint-stock companies → trade post emps.: Br in India, Dutch in Indonesia • Dutch used violence to conquer spice-producing islands & achieved monopoly on spice trade • Br. est. trade posts in India w/ permission from (and payments to) Mughal govt.→ cotton export	• Like Dutch, Br ↑ wealth & power b/c Asian "carrying" trade, even dealing bulk goods → mass market i.e. tea & textiles (not just luxury goods) • 7 Yrs' War: British defeat French in global conflict • 1757: Battle of Plassey—British East India Co. defeated Nawab of Bengal (India), est. control over this territory, paving way for full colonization • 1757: Canton System—Chinese limit European merchants to trade via 1 port (Canton)

If your first thought was that these organizers look like old-school "cheat sheets," you're right! There's a reason why History teachers still use a tried-and-true method like the knowledge organizer: it works. This document is a quick reference sheet for the major dates, historical actors, and events of the unit. By fitting all that information into a small amount of space you also encourage visual memory to help the knowledge retention. In the end, a cheat sheet serves its purpose: to cheat knowledge loss.

Core Idea

Cheat knowledge loss with cheat sheets.

Some may worry that these knowledge organizers do all the work for students. We prefer to think about it this way: by giving knowledge organizers to students, teachers

Build Knowledge   71

can shift in-class time from passive copying to active engagement, and from knowledge retrieval to actual historical analysis. As students practice using the knowledge contained within the organizer, the act of recall encourages memory formation.

Other ways to encourage internalization include assigning homework or writing prompts that require the organizer for completion and using the organizer as a study tool for class oral reviews or quizzes. Some teachers have found success by providing partially completed organizers and having students fill out the rest during the lesson.

Rachel also uses the organizer to fill in gaps for students. For example, if students struggle to name or use essential background knowledge within a given lesson, Rachel directs them to the knowledge organizer. This move keeps the thinking on the student, not Rachel. Sharing the resource helps Rachel drive learning, while also clueing students in on what to prioritize. It's the History class version of the math/science formula sheet.

Classroom notes are another resource Rachel promotes. As students write about or debate the day's essential question, they can refer to their own notes to bolster arguments-in-the-making (more on that later).

Knowledge organizers, homework, and notebooks can remind students to activate knowledge they might not otherwise use—but it doesn't build knowledge they've never had.

FRONTLOAD KNOWLEDGE—TELL A STORY

While reading historical documents will be a main driver of knowledge acquisition (as we saw in Part 1), students will never have enough time in class to learn all the historical knowledge they need just from sources. There will be times when a teacher needs to supplement learning with a direct teaching move called frontloading. In *Uncommon Core*, Smith, Appleman, and Wilhelm name frontloading as key time to share information—before students need to use it.[11]

Let's watch Rachel frontload knowledge after activating knowledge with the Do Now and Knowledge Organizer.

Build Knowledge Lesson

European Exploration—A Snippet of the Lesson

RACHEL: Frankopan opens this chapter of *The Silk Roads* by stating, "the world changed in the late 15th century." Of course, we know that 1492 marked a crucial turning point as Columbus encountered the Americas. But as you've read in Frankopan, Columbus intended to sail to India. Why? We're going to add some important historical context to our notes on the causes and impacts of European exploration in the 15th century.

[PPT Slide with an image and simple words: "Spices trade—European demand and Muslim control"]

According to Tom Standage in *An Edible History of Humanity*, Europe's high demand for spices imported from Asia (pepper, cloves, cinnamon, and ginger) made the spice trade a lucrative business. Spices were a commodity (an agricultural product that could be bought or sold) for which European customers were willing to pay high prices. Without it, food was pretty tasteless. Here's the catch: by the 15th century, Muslim traders had gained a significant stake in the spice trade market, which concerned Europeans. These traders worked closely with Venetians to distribute the spices to the wider European market. Although the Catholic Church attempted to disrupt this trade link by banning trade with the Muslim world, the Venetians found workarounds or ignored these mandates. Muslim influence in the region continued to increase as the Ottoman Turks began to take over territories formally controlled by the crumbling Byzantine Empire. The years 1410–1414 marked a sharp spike in the cost of imported spices. English consumers, for example, found that pepper was eight times as expensive as it used to be. This inflation prompted Europe to more seriously consider ways to establish direct trade relationships with Asia through new trade routes unknown to Muslim traders. Europe realized in a very painful way how dependent they were on suppliers. You might have noticed something similar in oil prices recently.

Pause for a moment and consider this question: *How might European leaders respond to the rising cost of luxury goods? What actions could they take?*

Turn and talk with your table partner to discuss . . .

[After Rachel brings the class back together as a whole group, she solicits a few ideas.]

Let's see what happened!

[Rachel then clicks to a new slide about Reconquista and Asian navigational technology and continues her lecture.]

You probably noticed one thing immediately: unlike every other classroom example thus far, in this one, student voice is minimized. The teacher is doing most of the talking—it sounds like a glorified lecture. Yet Rachel is trying to do more than that. How?

Consider this. Recall a highly engaging novel that you read recently or as a youth, like the Harry Potter series. It likely takes little effort to bring it to mind, even if it's been years since you've thought of it. You might not remember every detail, but you can recall the arc of the story, dozens of characters and plot lines, and the ending. Now think about your car insurance policy—often 30 pages long. A Harry Potter novel is 500 pages, yet you probably remember much more from there than from a much shorter document. Why is Harry Potter easier to recall? The human mind is built for narrative. Stories make knowledge stick.

> ## Core Idea
> The human mind is built for narrative. Stories make knowledge stick.

For much of human history, oral storytelling has been a primary way to encode and share knowledge. We still seek stories today, albeit in a wider range of formats. Movies, novels, podcasts, sporting events, and even trial proceedings all use storytelling to influence how we absorb information.[12] Why does this matter to History teachers? Stories make great instructional aids. Neuroscientists note that "storytelling engages not just people's intellect, but also their feelings: a bald recitation of facts invariably lacks the impact (and the enduring power) of a coherent narrative that awakens one's emotion."[13] When we engage with story, multiple areas of information processing in the brain are activated. The chemicals that are released, like cortisol, dopamine, and oxytocin, "attach" to elements of the story, making these memories more charged and easier to recall over time than non-narrative information.[14]

Zaretta Hammond, author of *Culturally Responsive Teaching and the Brain*, notes that students from more collectivist cultures and/or cultures with strong oral traditions are uniquely primed to respond to storytelling as a mode of learning, as this is a common method of information delivery in their culture.[15] For educators teaching students from a wide range of backgrounds, storytelling is a powerful teaching move to level the playing field and benefit all learners.

Nowhere is the idea of storytelling more important than in History class. The past is chockful of background knowledge: dates, times, names, places. But teaching it as a list assigns this schema the same level of importance as a line in an insurance policy—quickly noted, not always understood, and even more quickly forgotten. Taking that same historical context and shaping it into a narrative changes the game. A structured story helps students organize background knowledge in a meaningful way. And what they can organize, they can remember.

The power of story goes beyond simple remembering of the past—it is the platform on which students can make sense of it. With the right story, students will have a greater ability to analyze, dissect, and critique historical moments.

In recent decades, direct instruction moves like storytelling have fallen out of fashion. They've been replaced by more student-driven design, like flipped classrooms, where teachers serve more as facilitators than as "sages on the stage." Putting more learning in students' hands is a good thing, but as with any pendulum swing in education, the best location is near the middle. We deeply believe in the power of inquiry (as we'll discuss in the next chapters) and yet we won't get as far without strategically leveraging knowledge building as well to create the most powerful learning outcomes. In the best storytelling, there is still room to incorporate student voice and active thinking in a meaningful and intentional way. As we saw in the snapshot from Rachel's lesson, she strategically incorporates engaging turn-and-talk questions that encourage students to make predictions, respond to shocking moments in the story, or check for understanding of what they just learned.

So what converts a teacher presentation from the equivalent of a dry read of an insurance policy to an enthralling, memorable story? Hook them, tell the story, and guide them to hold onto it.

Hook Them

Connect Yesterday to Today

Come with us to Cat Lum's 11th-grade US History class. Students have been studying the causes of agrarian discontent between 1800 and 1900, and Cat sees an opportunity to connect the economic concerns of 19th-century to those of modern-day Midwestern factory workers. Watch what she does next.

WATCH Clip 3: Cat Lum—Opening Hook (Gilded Age)

Sample Hook—Causes of 19th-century Agrarian Discontent

CAT (TEACHER): So I want to draw a quick modern connection to what we're studying today. Take a look at this slide. We're looking at the presidential election results from November [2020]. Red is depicting what political party?

STUDENTS: Republicans.

CAT (TEACHER): And blue is depicting?

STUDENTS: Democrats.

CAT (TEACHER): So when we're looking at the map, what part of the country did we see flock toward the Republican party that we didn't see before?

STUDENT: The Midwest.

CAT (TEACHER): Social scientists and likely future historians are looking at why these Midwestern voters flocked toward the Republican Party. What were they concerned about or fearful of?

[Students talk in pairs about potential causes of the voter bloc shift. When time is up, Cat calls on a student to share out to the full class.]

STUDENT: They wanted to be compensated with factory jobs because under Obama's presidency they didn't have those jobs anymore.

CAT (TEACHER): Great. Anything else you guys want to add? [Pauses]. So a big part of this is going to be an economic concern, and I want to draw a connection to what we've seen in the Gilded Age. We have an economic concern, both today from a lot of farmers and other Midwesterners who are looking for those jobs to be reopened, as well as during the Gilded Age. Farmers are in debt during this time period; they're looking for a way out. Today we're going to talk about the economic situation these farmers were facing and what they were trying to do to mitigate this problem, which brings us to our inquiry question. . . .

Cat uses the 2020 election results to underscore a thread of continuity that may link two seemingly disparate groups (19th-century farmers and 21st-century factory workers). Through a thought-provoking prompt and short discussion, Cat and her students raised the possibility that economic anxieties may have at least partially contributed to the rise of each of these movements. Launching the lesson by emphasizing common denominators across time helps students recognize the patterns that drive historical developments, thus making the distant past, as unique as it may have been, more familiar.

Making a contemporary link is one way to hook students into a lesson. Jillian shows us another.

Immerse Yourself in the Drama of Yesterday

The students in Jillian's 11th-grade AP US History have just completed a unit on the progress and limitations of the Reconstruction period in America and the subsequent rise of Jim Crow segregation in the South. They are about to begin a lesson about how two of the leading Black intellectuals, Booker T. Washington and W.E.B. Du Bois, sought to challenge and undermine the systems of racism in America. How does Jillian's move engage students in the day's essential question?

 WATCH Clip 4: Jillian Gaeta—Opening Hook (Reconstruction)

Sample Hook—Reconstruction Priorities

JILLIAN (TEACHER): So during this time, African Americans are facing all these issues [points to board] after Reconstruction. As an activist during this time, you're faced with some tough decisions. You're not sure what is the most important thing to prioritize, or how you need to tackle all these issues. If you were an activist during this time, what would be the most important issue for you to prioritize?

[Written on Jillian's Do Now list: lynching, education rights, restriction on political freedom, increase in segregation, black codes, injustice in law, lack of economic rights.]
[Several students share out the issue they would prioritize. Education, lynching, and segregation are each mentioned, but no single answer draws the majority of students' support.]

JILLIAN (TEACHER): What is the problem arising in our classroom that would have been a problem in 1877?

ERIN: People were split on what the most important problem was, and they didn't know what they should handle first. Du Bois and Washington were conflicted with each other.

JILLIAN (TEACHER): Yes. So today we are going to look at how Booker T. Washington and Du Bois differed on their opinions and ideologies in how to deal with these issues. Just as we saw in this class, there were divisions among African Americans in how to deal with them.

Jillian's words plug students directly into the day's inquiry. Not only does her question connect to prior knowledge recalled in the Do Now, but it builds historical empathy by asking students to consider a past dilemma within the context of their own lives. If you want to hook students, make a connection.

By asking students to consider some of the real challenges that the African American community was facing, and by taking it a step further by asking them to prioritize how those challenges should be addressed, Jillian puts students in the center of the historical debate. While Jillian's students live in a very different time than that of Booker T. Washington and Du Bois at the turn of the 20th century, there are still connections that can be made to make the past feel a little less foreign. The ensuing discussion organically leads to the prompt, which is an examination of two different avenues for African American progress as advocated for by Du Bois and Washington.

Another type of hook relies on mystery to pique students' interest. Let's investigate.

Create Mystery—Contrast Setting and Outcome

Bassett and Shiffman of 4QM advocate contrasting setting and outcome to create a sense of mystery. In the case of Rachel's World History class, here is another hook that she used earlier in the unit.

Sample Hook—Colonization of the Americas

RACHEL: In 1492, the Americas were ruled by their native peoples, some in enormous and powerful empires. One hundred years later, those empires had been conquered by foreigners who would transform the economy, culture, and even geography of the continent. How did THAT happen? Let's find out.

This condensed form of storytelling engages students' curiosity. It establishes a setting (the pre-Colombian societies of the Americas) that is dramatically changed (outcome) by the arrival of Europeans. For the students in Rachel's class, the question "How did that happen?" becomes a call to action that will guide their learning: how they absorb frontloaded knowledge, what prior knowledge they will use, and the historical thinking skills they will leverage to respond to the prompt in full.

Problematize—Create Tension

Let's return to the hook that Rachel used to launch her lesson. She took a slightly different tactic, this time creating tension by problematizing the Westernization narrative.

Build Knowledge Lesson

Lesson: Interrogating the "Rise of the West"

[Students turn and talk with a peer for 1 minute: what do they think is Westernization. Then Rachel calls them together and they share ideas of culture, political and economic influence, and power.]

RACHEL (TEACHER):   Fascinating. So we have a lot of ideas associated with this term. Today, we are going to build on that knowledge and go deeper. You see, historians have often labeled this period as "The Rise of the West": when Europe starts to expand its power and influence, not only in America but across the globe. These historians might argue that this Rise of the West is exemplified by Columbus's voyage and the subsequent European colonization of the Americas.

But something fascinating has happened in just the past 20 years. Historians have gotten into a massive debate: Should we consider the end of the 15th century as the rise of the West and beginning of global westernization? Or should we see it differently? I'm not going to decide this answer: you are. But first you need to meet the historians on all sides of this debate. And you need a bit of knowledge to make your assessment.

Please take a look at the Knowledge Organizer in your Course Reader. I want to draw your attention to two terms that we will encounter today. . .

Problematizing is a technique that works in all aspects of teaching history (we'll see much more of it in discourse in Part 4). It opens up history to authentic debate, which is where the real acts of historical thinking occur. By hooking them into a debate, Rachel incentivizes her students to want to learn and/or activate needed prior knowledge to strengthen their arguments for the new learning to come.

Students are often more engaged in History class when they can see how the past connects to some aspect of their lives. But there doesn't need to be a one-to-one correlation to draw in students. A framing that speaks to universal issues, like freedom, invites students into discourse with the past. How do those seeking change in their communities, especially when lacking real political power, strategize and fight to enact change? Why might individuals, while fighting for the same final goal, still seek different paths to achieve it?

Seek Learning Connections—Leverage KWL Charts

Take a look at the following charts from Neha Marvania's 5th-grade Ancient World History class and Scott Kern's 11th-grade AP US History class. Each uses a KWL chart to launch the first lesson of a new unit. What do you notice?

Sample KWL Charts

5th-Grade Ancient World History—Ancient Egypt Unit

Essential Question:

Did Egyptian religion shape politics and culture or was it the other way around?

To determine this, we will be studying:

- Egyptian Mythology!
- The building of the pyramids!
- Mummies & the Afterlife!
- The role of the pharaohs!
- Writing & Math in Ancient Egypt!
- How Ancient Egyptians spent their lives every day!
- The beginning of the Jewish religion!

Know	Want to Know	Learned
Egypt was ruled by pharaohs	Who were famous pharaohs?	
When the pharaohs died, they were buried in pyramids as mummies	Why did they bury the pharaohs with treasure?	
Treasures were buried in the pyramids	What was their religion like?	
They write in hieroglyphs		

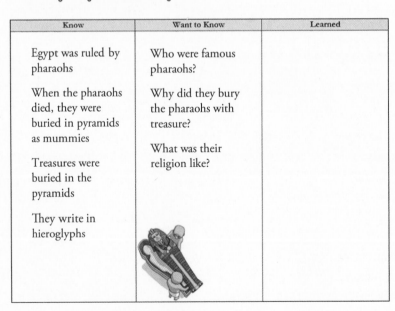

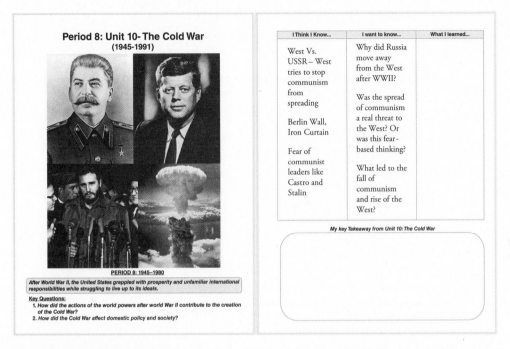

Source: (a): Wikimedia Commons / CC0 1.0; (b): NASA / Public Domain; (c): The Library of Congress / Wikimedia Commons / Public Domain; (d): U.S. National Archives and Records Administration (NARA) / Wikimedia Commons / Public Domain

In them you will notice three columns: K (What do I know already?), W (What do I want to know/learn?), and L (What have I learned from this unit?). The first two columns were filled out at the start of the lesson, and the last one at the end of the unit.

The K reaffirms what we already mentioned previously: activating knowledge reveals the context students already carry and surfaces misconceptions to be addressed. When students fill out the W column, they set a purpose for learning by deciding what they want to discover about the past. This learning connection builds purpose: I have something I want to get from this lesson. Students can turn and talk about their charts while the teacher charts some of the responses for the whole class. Art would often post a class KWL chart at the front of room and leave it up for the entirety of the unit as a visual reflection of learning-in-progress. A KWL chart not only makes learning connections but also is a useful aid to chronicle learning over time.

The *hook* is aptly named. In whatever style you choose, this quick teaching move takes only 3–5 minutes, but it ignites the interest for the students, making them more eager—and open—to learning.

A Note on Cultural Responsiveness and Anti-Racism

You might notice something in common among nearly all of the hooks presented here. They make history meaningful by stretching students to consider other perspectives. As the African proverb notes, "Until the lion learns to write, the story of the hunt will always glorify the hunter." These hooks resist the surety of a single story.

So does the discipline of historical thinking. By its nature, historical thinking requires looking at the past through multiple lenses and doing deep analysis—and it always has. Great historians of every age have evaluated and critiqued former interpretations of history.

The current polemic around anti-racism in education misses this historical understanding. At its essence, anti-racist instruction is honoring the need for viewing history from every lens and not simply the dominant narrative of the time. It would be irresponsible historical scholarship to do otherwise. Historical thinking also demands a frank assessment of the systems and structures of power and oppression of the time. That's why anti-racist teaching, which shows students how to recognize and transform these systems, is a key component to teaching history well. For example, teaching about the limitations and successes of Reconstruction is not just anti-racist; it is basic history—it teaches students to think and make sense of the past. Being culturally responsive means we think carefully about how to teach "hard" history, like the harrowing legacy of Jim Crow segregation, and how these lessons may impact the different students we teach. It requires that we as instructors and fellow historians reflect on who we are and how that could influence our instruction.

A community of teachers and school leaders came together to create a curriculum tool that teachers can use to evaluate the culturally responsive and equitable components of their lessons. We have included it the online Appendix.

Hooking students is the launch to effective storytelling (just like the cliffhangers at the end of novel chapters to get you to keep reading!). Now Rachel is ready to frontload new knowledge. Here she emphasizes the most important component of frontloading knowledge: rather than a series of events, tell a story, and make that story memorable.

Tell the Story—Make It Memorable

Step back and recall a moment when you listened to a standalone lecture that didn't stick. A number of factors could have contributed to the lackluster nature of the lecture.

When done poorly, history instruction can produce the same sensation. To avoid this, Rachel works on being an effective storyteller.

Build Bridges

Constructing the past as a cohesive narrative, rather than a collection of isolated facts, is challenging. This challenge is even more daunting when you are dealing with hundreds of years of history covered in a typical survey-level history class. How does Rachel help students see the links between given topics or units, drawing a line from a unit on Reconstruction in America to Western expansion or the Gilded Age? She build bridges: where you've been, where you are, and where you're going.

Core Idea

Tell a story by building bridges:
where you've been, where you are, and where you're going.

Building bridges is about helping students see the causation that underlies historical events and developments and gives motivation to historic actors. Students recognize the predictable beats of story (the who, what, when, where, and why, and how the previous era led to the next) and these become signposts to which they will attach related and new information.

Structuring or sequencing your units in a way that makes sense is less dependent on the curriculum plan and more on how you make that sequence explicit. Rachel uses the simple but effective sentence stems listed next to bridge units and lessons.

Language to Bridge Units

- "We recently ended a unit on *x* and explored *y*. In our new unit, we'll see how *z* approaches the same concept."
- "Both *x* and *y* civilizations experienced *z*."
- "Throughout this period of time, we have seen the trend of *x* emerge. This trend played out in a powerful way when we examined *y* during our last unit. Now let's see how this trend emerges in our new unit on *z*."

Keep It Short

With these bridges, Rachel launches into the full story that will give students the knowledge they need. While this is the heart of frontloading knowledge, she still keeps her story relatively short—10 minutes (starting at shorter amounts of time for younger students and moving up progressively for older students). This keeps teacher talk to a minimum and gives time for students to do the more important work: internalize the knowledge for themselves. The habit of note-taking helps them hold onto what they've learned.

Hold onto the Story—Solidify the Understanding

The end goal of a Build Knowledge lesson is that students are equipped with the needed knowledge of the time period to be able to do document analysis and generate their own plausible theses. To do that, students have to be able to hold onto the story you shared and remember what happened.

A great question to ask yourself as a history teacher is, what will students have at their disposal to remember that lesson? Rachel uses the following strategies to help students hold onto the learning.

Build Note-Taking Habits

When you think of understanding, ask yourself this question: What will students study from when they prepare for a midterm or final?

One of the easiest ways to answer that is looking at student notes. You can judge a lot about the quality of the preparation from the quality of a student's notebook.

Core Idea

A measure of knowledge building is the quality of students' notebooks.

Detailed notes create a powerful resource for knowledge retrieval that students will be able to use throughout the year. This is also a fundamental skill for students to carry with them beyond high school, where most college classes are dominated by lectures. Yet if you peruse the notebooks of a typical class of students, you'll find a big disparity across the quality of notes—often correlating to the difference in their achievement on upcoming assessments. Teachers like Rachel don't leave notebook skills to chance (or only to those who already are equipped); they create the habits.

At the beginning of the year, Rachel formally teaches note-taking to her students (she happens to use Cornell Notes, but any system can work). As Rachel talks, students use Cornell Notes to capture the story.

Sample—Student's Notes

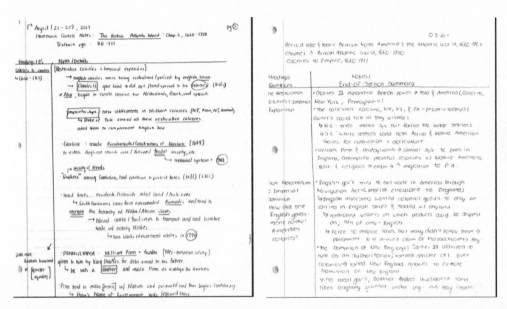

Note: A full-size version of these Cornell notes can be found in the Online Content at the beginning of the book in the "Appendix—Print-Ready Materials" section, along with several other examples.

How does Rachel ensure that all her students have notes like these? She follows a few simple steps:

1. Indicate to the students when it is time to take notes.

2. While speaking, look around the room to make sure students are taking notes; redirect them if they are not.

3. Make notes an active listening task by *not* sharing all the written notes on the board/projector. Rather, just provide a few key phrases/visual anchors to accompany your story. Remind them to write down what they hear, not just what's on the board.

4. Put them to use: let them see their notes are immediately useful by giving them an immediate task to check for understanding (a turn and talk to compare notes, a quick open-notes quiz, etc.).

Taking systematic notes can be a game-changer for students' knowledge retention. Rachel makes sure of this by putting them to use.

Put Notebooks to Use

After frontloading knowledge and asking students to take notes, Rachel monitors how well students can retell the story. About halfway through the presentation, she asks a quick question to monitor comprehension about the narrative so far, then walks around to see what notes students have captured and to listen to students as they discuss in pairs and small groups. The responses let her know if she has to address earlier parts of the lecture or if she can move forward to tell the remainder of the story.

At the end of her story, she provides an additional opportunity to check for understanding. While there are myriad options, two high-leverage ways are listed here.

Write a Four-Sentence Summary

To ensure that a story contains all the essential elements, Bassett and Shiffman recommend boiling it down to a four-sentence summary.[16] Following is one for the well-known story of the American Revolutionary War.

Four-Sentence Summary for the American Revolutionary War

1. British/colonial tension continued to mount as new taxes/acts were passed like the Coercive Acts in 1774, and new more intense forms of resistance by the colonists like the Boston Tea Party in 1773 emerged.

2. Despite forming a Continental Congress and attempting to make peace with Britain, open conflict broke out at the Battles of Lexington and Concord in 1775.

3. Despite overwhelming odds, the Americans, under the leadership of George Washington, defeated the British with the help of the French and signed the Treaty of Paris, officially ending the war in 1783.

4. The unlikely victory over the British Empire resulted in American independence. The question remained whether this new, democratic nation could effectively be governed and live up to the Enlightenment ideals expressed in Thomas Jefferson's Declaration of Independence.

A strong four-sentence summary contains a specific setting, historic actors, time period, and describes a change.[17] This summary contains all of these.

Take a moment and try it yourself. Consider one of your upcoming lessons where you need to frontload knowledge for your students. Tell the story of that lesson in four sentences, and then take a moment to reflect on the process.

Stop & Jot: A Four-Sentence Summary

1.

2.

3.

4.

Stop & Jot

What was the process like for you?

_____

_____

_____

Summarizing distills thinking. A single glance at a student's paper shows Rachel what historical context is "sticky" and what needs to be reinforced.

There is another, more visual way to retell the story—the six-panel storyboard.

Create a Six-Panel Storyboard

For Scott's unit on Civil War and Reconstruction, he chose to do a storyboard instead of a summary. Bassett and Shiffman recommend using these six panels to consolidate narrative in a more condensed way. What do you notice about it?

Six-Panel Storyboard Sample: 1861–1896

Civil War	President Versus Congress	Terror
• Confederacy versus Union	• Thaddeus Stevens	• Redeemers
• Emancipation Proclamation	• Radical Republicans	• KKK
• Ulysses S. Grant	• Andrew Johnson	• Black Codes
• Assassination	• Impeachment	• Sharecropping
Radical Reconstruction	**Reconstruction Ends**	**Resistance**
• Grant	• Compromise of 1877	• Booker T. Washington
• Reconstruction Amendments	• Poll tax, literacy test, grandfather clause	• W.E.B. Dubois
• Freedmen's Bureau	• *U.S. vs Cruikshank*	• Ida B. Wells
• Civil Rights Act	• Plessy v. Ferguson	• NAACP
	• Jim Crow	

The story starts with a specific setting (the Civil War) and ends with a series of changes, including the 1896 *Plessy v. Ferguson* decision that followed the end of Reconstruction and the beginning of legally sanctioned segregation in the South. Each box captures a major beat in the narrative, for example, "the Civil War" and the relevant schema needed to access it. Just as authors and directors do, Scott uses this structure to visualize and gut-check that the essential, sequential schema of the story has been captured.

Every method for checking for understanding requires some instruction for students to complete independently, with the six-panel storyboard often taking a little longer for students to get the hang of. Although it appears to be an easier task because it requires less writing, students still have to think critically to fill in the boxes. Not only do they have to determine the most important elements of the story but they also have to sort them into relevant categories and title them. Most students will likely prefer one method of summarizing over another. Scott uses both when he teaches; they are excellent ways to capture in-progress student thinking at the end of the lesson.

CONCLUSION

To see the fruit of building knowledge, let's return to Rachel's classroom. A few weeks have passed since the lessons and materials shared at the beginning in the chapter, and students are preparing to discuss the essential question of the unit, "Is 1498 better understood as the beginning of 'Westernization' or a continuation of 'Southernization'?" Here is a snapshot of part of the discussion.

Class Discussion—Southernization or Westernization?

RACHEL (TEACHER): Okay, based on the evidence that you and your peers analyzed, is 1498 better understood as the beginning of "Westernization" or a continuation of "Southernization"?

ADAM: I think the Early Modern Era should be understood as a continuation of Southernization because Europe's rise to power was built upon developments that originated in South Asia.

JORDAN: I agree with Adam—we see evidence of this in Shaffer's article. Much of the technology that powered European exploration and conquest originated in South Asia, including new navigational technology, gunpowder, printing, and the crystallization of sugar. Without these technological achievements, Westernization would not have been possible.

BRIANNA: But wait, are we really minimizing the influence of the West in the early modern era? The Early Modern Era—beginning with the voyages of Columbus and Da Gama—marked the start of a process of "Westernization" due to the spread of European languages and Christianity to Asia and the Americas. The conquest and colonization of the Americas is clear evidence that 1498 represents the beginning of Westernization, not Southernization.

With knowledge, real multifaceted analysis becomes possible—students go from a single argument to multiple. Our role, then, is simply to encourage them to do so. What does it take to move students from telling the story to analyzing it? We'll show how in Part 3: Grapple with Evidence.

KEY TAKEAWAYS

- Take the ordinary and make it extraordinary by building up their knowledge.
- The difference between what we forget and what we remember is knowledge retrieval.
- Activating knowledge activates the brain: you make connections between what you already know and what you're about to learn.
- Class oral review embeds knowledge into long-term memory.

- Cheat knowledge loss with cheat sheets.
- The human mind is built for narrative. Stories make knowledge stick.
- What we can organize, we can remember.
- Hook students by making connections.
- Tell a story by building bridges: where you've been, where you are, and where you're going.
- A measure of knowledge building is the quality of students' notebooks.

BUILD KNOWLEDGE LESSON ONE-PAGER

Prepare	Before Instruction

	Identify the knowledge students need:
	• Review the sources of your Inquiry Lesson:
	   ○ What knowledge can students glean on their own from their reading?
	   ○ What knowledge do they need in order to understand and analyze the sources?
	• Plan your lesson to build only the essential knowledge needed (see following).

Activate Knowledge 5–15 min	**Launch the Class**
	Do Now: • Review of spiraled content and/or skill that is needed for the lesson OR. • Cornell notes quiz on previous content and/or HW assignment—assess basic comprehension. **Class oral review:** • Spiral relevant content that directly connects to the day's lesson (leverage the unit Knowledge Organizer). • Spiral key concepts and vocabulary of previous content (not necessarily relevant to this specific lesson).

Hook 2–5 min	Tell a Memorable Story

	Hook them:
	• Build a bridge—connect the topic to one of the following:
	   ◦ Cultural relevance
	   ◦ Students' lives
	   ◦ Prior knowledge
	   ◦ An enduring understanding
	• Sell it—model engagement and enthusiasm for the content by:
	   ◦ Heightened inflection (use dramatic pauses, punch key questions)
	   ◦ Vocal/facial expression (communicate passion and intrigue).
	• Ask a turn-and-talk question to add student voice.

Tell the Story
10–20 min
	Set the stage:
	• Have students turn to a new page in their notebook and title it accordingly.
	Tell the story:
	• Focus on knowledge that goes beyond what students would be able to know/do independently (through their reading or use of a knowledge organizer).
	• Keep slides sparse:
	   ◦ Have little text so students focus on listening during note-taking, not simply copying the slides.
	• Make the story memorable:
	   ◦ Make it a cohesive story rather than disparate facts: connect one part to the other.

Check for Understanding 15–20 min	Check for Understanding

	Monitor:
	• Monitor student note-taking:
	   ◦ Highlight strong notes.
	   ◦ Prompt students to elaborate where notes are sparse.
	Check for understanding:
	• Peer-to-peer:
	   ◦ Team up students to review notes with each other and fill in gaps.
	• Individually:
	   ◦ Draft 4-sentence summary or 6-panel storyboard.
	• Class oral review:
	   ◦ Ask key questions to check for their understanding of the lecture.
	   ◦ Chart for reference.
	Exit ticket:
	• Monitor student work to identify trends.

SELF-ASSESSMENT

Part 2: Build Knowledge	
Activate Knowledge	__/ 10
• Do Nows, class oral reviews, and resources (e.g., knowledge organizers)	
Frontload Knowledge	__/ 10
• Hook them and make the story memorable.	
• Build note-taking habits.	
• Have a clear check-for-understanding activity (e.g., four-sentence summary, six-panel storyboard, etc.).	
Part 2 Score:	____/20

PLANNING FOR ACTION

• Which key ideas from this section resonate the most for you?

• How will you take and/or modify these resources to meet the needs of your class(es)?

_____

_____

_____

Action	Date

Part 3

Grapple with Evidence

"Education must enable one to sift and weigh evidence, to discern the true from the false, the real from the unreal, and the facts from the fiction. The function of education, therefore, is to teach one to think intensively and to think critically."

—Dr. Martin Luther King Jr.

"History is the attempt to recreate and explain the significant features of the past on the basis of fragmentary and imperfect evidence."

—Terry Crowley

In the 1960s in New York City, police raids at gay bars were quite common. Crowd resistance wasn't.

On June 28, 1969, eight plainclothes officers had no trouble getting into the Stonewall Inn, an iconic gay bar in the city. The trouble was they couldn't get out: The crowd refused to disperse. The bar's displaced LGBTQ patrons and employees had lined the street since the start of the early morning raid, and onlookers joined as the news spread. When an additional police unit began to load the detained in a van, the crowd's anger boiled over. From somewhere in the crowd, a penny arced across the summer air. "Here's your payoff, you pigs!"

More coins and other objects flew. They zinged against the windows of the police vehicle and clattered against the sidewalk. The original officers inside the now-empty bar scanned the space. They would need to barricade the door—and quickly.

What happened over the course of the next few days was completely out of the ordinary. Up until that point, most LGBTQ Americans had kept a low profile. Being publicly out or outed carried great risk: job and/or housing loss, arrest, or even death. This long history of explicit persecution spiked during the Lavender Scare of the 1950s, when the government dismissed thousands of federal employees for their orientation. The challenges continued in the 1960s. In New York City alone, many practices were overtly hostile toward the LGBTQ population: the solicitation of same-sex relations was illegal, same-sex dancing was prohibited, and the New York State Liquor Authority shut down and denied licenses to places that served alcohol to known or suspected members of the community. The mafia came to operate most gay bars and regularly bribed police officers to keep them open. The police, in turn, often harassed these bars for their patronage and mafia connection.

Yet on this night, the LGTBQ community did not stay quiet—they struck back. For the next six days the Stonewall riot (or uprising) would continue. (Whether to call this a riot or an uprising is part of the sense-making of this unit: students will decide which term feels more apt, as they will encounter both terms in the sources.)

The events of Stonewall raise intriguing questions: What made the Stonewall Inn ripe for an uprising in 1969? Though Stonewall did not mark the beginning of the gay liberation movement, many historians view it as a galvanizing moment of LGBTQ political activism that led to the foundation of future LGBTQ activist organizations. Why then and there?

Courtney's 11th-grade US history students dove into the question posed by this Stanford History Education Group lesson.[1] Let's listen in.

Class Discussion

Lesson: Causes of the Stonewall Uprising in 1969

COURTNEY (TEACHER): Okay, so after reading the evidence that we have in front of us, and after your small-group discussions, what caused the Stonewall riots in 1969? Who'd like to begin?

CHRIS:	I think the riots started because the LGBTQ community in Greenwich was just tired of the harassment. Dick Leitsch mentions in Source 3 in the first line how police had been targeting gay bars in NYC and that several had been raided and closed because they didn't have liquor licenses. It seems like they were tired of the harassment.
ALEX:	Yeah, I can build on that. Source 1, from the *NY Daily News*, also described how the Stonewall was operating without a liquor license and was therefore targeted by police. So that corroborates the trend that Chris noted about these bars being targeted by police.
DANA:	I agree. The homophobia of the time was probably just too much. These people were gathering and peacefully socializing, only to have their community targeted.
COURTNEY (TEACHER):	This is interesting. Many of us are landing on this idea of pervasive homophobia being the key factor that led to the Stonewall riots. But homophobia and transphobia were not new phenomena in 1969. We talked about the Lavender Scare and the long history of discrimination and oppression faced by the LGBTQ community in America. And the NYC police had raided illegal bars before. So that alone doesn't explain this moment of resistance in 1969. Remember we can't explain a change—in this case, the Stonewall uprising—with a continuity—homophobia. We can only explain a change with a change. I want you to go back to your sources. Particularly focus on the point of view of each author and what was unique about that time and place.

[During a period of re-reading and small-group discussion, Courtney circulates and listens in. Five minutes pass, and she returns to large-group discussion and calls on three students she heard in the small groups.]

COURTNEY (TEACHER):	I heard some great small-group discussions. What do we think now? Let's hear some different perspectives from Blake, Kennedy, and Olu.
BLAKE:	Well, I think that we have to place this moment in the context of the Civil Rights movement and the other protest movements of that time period.
COURTNEY (TEACHER):	Why do you say that? Please elaborate.
BLAKE:	Well, in Source 2, Sylvia Rivera's speech, who we know from our notes was one of the leaders of this uprising, was a participant in some of the other protest movements of the time, including the Civil Rights movement and the anti-war movement. Perhaps she and others saw this as a moment to take what they learned about resistance in those movements to use for their own cause and fight for equality.
KENNEDY:	I agree with Blake. Document 4, the Ladder article, connects to this idea of the influence of this era of protest because it describes how new organizations like the Mattachine Society of New York and the Homophile Youth Movement began leafletting the Village in order to organize protests against the conditions which sparked the riots. Protest and

	resistance seemed to be in the air at this time. Many of the activists and patrons of Stonewall were directly involved in other protest movements and even used similar strategies.
OLU:	I somewhat agree with you, but I think we need to look at the political context as well. We see in that same article that the police had always been corrupt in taking bribes from the bar owners, but a new precinct captain arrived who wanted to be seen as "tough on crime." He didn't realize what he was walking into and without his change in policy, the protest wouldn't have happened.
COURTNEY (TEACHER):	Thank you, Blake, Kennedy, and Olu. Let's definitely add that to our notes. Is there any other context that we might want to consider? And is there any other evidence that corroborates or presents a different account of what may have happened?

What a remarkable moment to watch unfold. Courtney wasn't satisfied with the initial simplistic and one-sided understanding of a historical moment. Yet with a few critical, strategic moves, the students' arguments and analysis grew into something more sophisticated. What stands out is that Courtney didn't do the heavy lifting to get there—the students did. All she had to do was get them to grapple with evidence.

> ## Core Idea:
> When you want them to get it, get them to grapple with evidence.

At the heart of historical thinking is the ability—and the desire—to grapple with evidence. Put pieces of evidence side by side, unpack them, and then make a judgment as to what happened or why or how it happened. In Courtney's classroom, the evidence is the source, not the teacher, which makes students the historians rather than observers of a historian. With this shift, they experience the fruit of grappling—and growing—on their path to making sense of history.

So, what do teachers like Courtney do to set up and facilitate moments like this? They don't just react to them; they anticipate them.

PLAN FOR PRODUCTIVE STRUGGLE

The Stonewall lesson contained four sources curated by SHEG. We'll dive into the second one, a speech by Sylvia Rivera given at a meeting of the Latino Gay Men of

New York, a community organization. Born and raised in New York City, Sylvia Rivera participated in the Stonewall Riots as a teenager. In her speech, Rivera describes the participation of transgender people across multiple movements in the 1960s. As Courtney prepared to teach this lesson, she asked herself, what might students miss in an initial reading? Consider the same as you read Rivera's words.

Unpacking a Source

Speech – Sylvia Rivera[2]

Source: Sylvia Rivera, speech to the Latino Gay Men of New York, June 2001. Reprinted in Centro Journal, Spring 2007.

We were all involved in different struggles, including myself and many other transgender people. But in these struggles, in the civil rights movement, in the war movement, in the women's movement, we were still outcasts. The only reason they tolerated the transgender community in some of these movements was because we were gung-ho, we were frontliners. We didn't take no shit from nobody. We had nothing to lose. . . . We were all in the bar, having a good time. Lights flashed on, we knew what was coming; it's a raid. . . . The routine was that the cops get their payoff, they confiscate the liquor . . . a padlock would go on the door. What we did, back then, was disappear to a coffee shop or any place in the neighborhood for fifteen minutes. You come back, the Mafia was there cutting the padlock off, bringing in more liquor, and back to business as usual. . . . The confrontation started outside by throwing change at the police. We started with the pennies, the nickels, the quarters, and the dimes. "Here's your payoff, you pigs!" . . . Once word of mouth got around that the Stonewall had gotten raided, and that there's a confrontation going on, people came from the clubs. But we have to remember one thing: that it was not just the gay community and the street queens that really escalated this riot; it was also the help of the many radical straight men and women that lived in the Village at that time, that knew the struggle of the gay community and the trans community. . . . So then the tactical police force came and heads were being bashed left and right. But what I found very impressive that evening, was that the more that they beat us, the more we went back for. We were determined that evening that we were going to be a liberated, free community.

Stop & Jot:

What do you think students might miss in an initial reading?

_____

_____

_____

_____

Let's see what Courtney thought: here is what she highlighted.

Courtney's Annotations of the Article

We were all involved in different struggles, including myself and many other transgender people. But in these struggles, in the Civil Rights movement, in the war movement, in the women's movement, we were still outcasts. The only reason they tolerated the transgender community in some of these movements was because we were gung-ho, we were frontliners. We didn't take no shit from nobody.[2]

Courtney knows that part of the historical thinking she wants her students to do is to place this seminal event within a larger historical context by examining how the changing conditions in New York City and nationwide might explain why activists chose this moment to fight back against the corruption and abuse of local law enforcement. In the case of the Stonewall uprising, Courtney anticipated that students might stay at a surface level of analysis and merely argue that the blatant homophobia evident in many of the documents could be used to explain the change in behavior as characterized by the patrons' revolt at the Stonewall Inn. What they could miss is that many of the key activists, like Sylvia, already had experience in the Civil Rights movement that they could draw on to mobilize protests at Stonewall. It is also noteworthy that as a transgender activist, Sylvia felt excluded from so many other movements that she could be more motivated by this one that felt closer to home. That context helps students understand some potential answers to the question "why here and now?"

Why was this pre-work so critical for Courtney? It enabled her to prepare for students' struggle, rather than eliminate it. If you return to the discourse at the opening of the chapter, you will note that she just states the problem (students missing the change), and asks students to re-read. Why? She knows that the magic of growth lies in productive struggle.

Core Idea

The magic of growth lies in productive struggle.

Consider the budding guitarist who wants to move from beginner to intermediate. Hours of practicing the same scales won't improve their skill, but choosing a melody slightly more difficult than what they can already play will. Or say you wanted to run your first marathon. Most coaches would advise against completing the entire 26.2 miles on your first run—you'd likely end that session exhausted and demoralized (and potentially injured). Better results are achieved by building stamina over time through increasingly longer runs. Success arrives not from avoiding struggle, but from making it productive.

Core Idea

Don't avoid the struggle. Make it productive.

Research shows that when students work at the edge of their current abilities, they increase their capacity for deeper thinking.[3] The key is to make sure the struggle remains within their zone of development.[4] Ask them to play a concerto without a single piano lesson, for example, and the struggle will be completely unproductive.

Productive struggle also increases engagement. Students become the problem-solvers: they don't wait for the teacher to solve it for them.

To identify a potential productive struggle in this lesson, Courtney needed a deep understanding of the question itself. What caused the Stonewall riot in Greenwich Village, New York in 1969? On the surface, this seems like a fairly straightforward cause-and-effect question. But closer examination reveals that the question is driving at what 4QM calls a Question 3 Historical Inquiry: "Why then and there?" Historical questions like these ask us to step back to consider the unique underlying factors and conditions that enable a particular event or story to play out in a specific way at a specific time and place. Answering "why then and there" requires us to place historical events within a proper historical context. Students need to identify a change or a difference in behavior or decision-making and then connect it to a change or difference in context and conditions.[5]

Courtney had already primed herself to find the challenge in the lesson with the creation of her original know-show chart (recall Jah'Nique's work in Part 1). She had answered the question for herself, "If they don't get this, they won't get that"—and realized that students might not catch the important context of a corrupt police force and changing precinct leadership.

A Note on Inflammatory Sources

When you study primary and secondary sources, you will likely run into certain sources that use inflammatory language. In this case, a NY Daily News piece by Jerry Lisker (Source 1) used inflammatory language to describe the LGBTQ patrons of Stonewall. Facing History and Our Selves provides useful guidance to educators on how to address dehumanizing language in sources that students encounter in class. In general, we recommend explicitly identifying instances of dehumanizing language and unpacking their context and impact in a thoughtful way with students. To do this well requires us as educators to spend the necessary time reflecting and unpacking our own biases, widening our own cultural aperture, as Zaretta Hammond would say, so that we can prepare to effectively and responsibly lead students through this work.[6]

For more strategies on how to address dehumanizing language in historical sources, please visit www.facinghistory.com.

Knowing where students might struggle is half the battle. Making the struggle productive is the second half.

SET THE STAGE—ACTIVATE WHAT THEY NEED

Having planned where she wants students to deepen their thinking, Courtney structures the start of the lesson to give students the essential tools they'll need to meet the challenge. But what if students don't yet have the necessary skills? Teachers like Courtney devote the start of the lesson to building them.

Build Skill with Guided Practice

One of the challenging skills in history class for middle and high school students is simply understanding what a question is asking you to do—and what knowledge you can apply to it. For most historians and history teachers, this skill has been so well practiced that it comes as second nature. This automaticity is not yet true for most of our students. We have to teach it to them.

Let's step into Art's 12th-grade AP US History class as he shows students the skill of breaking down and clarifying often-complex AP US History essay prompt. What do you notice about what he says and does?

Watch Clip 5: Art Worrell—Build Skill with Guided Practice

Think Aloud Teacher Model

Lesson: Breaking Down AP Essay Prompts

ART (TEACHER): We're going to look at an actual AP prompt from a topic that you should be pretty familiar with and I'm going to model my thinking for you about how I approach this particular prompt and how I begin to break it down. What I'd like you to do as I'm going through my thinking for this prompt is to record notes about any of the steps or questions that I ask myself to break down this prompt in an effective way. Just so that we're really clear, what are you actually taking notes on while I think aloud?

TAYLOR: We're taking notes on the strategies and basically the thinking that goes along with you breaking down an essay prompt.

ART (TEACHER): Great, don't worry so much about my annotations; I will provide those for you. Instead, focus more on the process and thinking behind each step I take. Okay, with that said, let's dive in. [Sets a timer]

ART (TEACHER): So, the first step I want to do is underline or circle the key words that signal the time and place of the prompt. [Reads the prompt aloud.] Historians have traditionally labeled the period after the War of 1812 the Era of Good Feelings. Evaluate the accuracy of this label, considering the emergence of nationalism and sectionalism. Use the documents and your knowledge of the period 1815–1825 to construct your response. Hmm . . . I see War of 1812 and Era of Good Feelings. Well, I know that the Era of Good Feelings was the time between 1815 and 1825. But the dates alone don't tell me much. I need to consider what is happening at that time that might help me to contextualize this prompt. Well I know that this Era of Good Feelings was characterized by increased nationalism, so I'm going to write nationalism in the margin. I also think of the Monroe Doctrine, which can be seen as another example of extreme nationalism, and served as a symbolic break from the colonial empires of the Old World and the shift toward the expansion of American democracy in the New World. That could be important context, so I'm noting it in the margins. Okay, that's all I can remember for now. The next thing I need to do is analyze the verb in the prompt so that I know what the task requires of me. The verb here is *evaluate* . . .

Art's moves give students an access ramp to more nuanced historical thinking. His think-aloud turns a complex, college-level prompt into a rigorous, yet achievable, task.

But Art doesn't just list a set of steps. He models the thinking, not just the procedure. That is what will help students activate those same mental processes themselves.

Core Idea

Model the thinking, not just the procedure.

Guided practice is how teachers like Art and Courtney explicitly teach historical strategy and skills to students. A strong teacher model is typically five to seven minutes in length and includes four or five easy-to-remember steps. The model is always followed by an opportunity for students to practice the skill, sometimes in isolation first and then in full implementation. In Art's class, he did a quick check for understanding of his think-aloud, then assigned a new prompt for students to unpack with a partner. Students broke down two more prompts in a final round of independent practice.

Gradually releasing responsibility through guided practice prepares students to independently handle the rigors of historical thinking. These skills may range from how to determine a claim or source a document to writing an argumentative essay. Guided practice offers an efficient way to introduce and practice discipline-specific skills. It is also an effective way to target and remediate disciplinary skills over the course of a year.

Once students have a solid foundation in a skill, you can simply activate it for the task at hand.

Activate Skill—Break Down the Prompt

Let's return to Courtney's class. How does she prepare students for the demands of the inquiry lesson?

Class Discussion—Breaking Down and Contextualizing the Prompt

COURTNEY (TEACHER): Who can read the historical question?

DREW: What caused the Stonewall riots in 1969?

COURTNEY (TEACHER): Thanks, Drew. Class, take a moment to silently re-read the prompt. What historical reasoning process will we be using today?

[Students read silently. Steven raises hand.]

STEVEN: Today we're using causation.

COURTNEY (TEACHER): That's right. And how can we organize our thinking when using causation?

JORDAN:	We can use a web diagram with the Stonewall riot in the middle and the factors as bubbles that feed into it.
COURTNEY (TEACHER):	Take a moment to start your web diagram with Stonewall at the center. We'll continue to build this diagram as we work through the sources. Now, as is the case with many causation prompts, which 4QM question type is this?
JAMES:	Question 3, because what it's really asking is why did the Stonewall riots happen at this time and place.
COURTNEY (TEACHER):	Great. So in addition to causation, we're also going to need to emphasize what reasoning process?
JAMES:	Contextualization, because we need to understand what was happening at that time and place that led to or made it possible for this event to happen.
COURTNEY (TEACHER):	Excellent! Well said, James. So, with that in mind, let's start to contextualize this prompt. What is happening in America in 1969 that may be relevant to this prompt? Take 3 minutes to independently brainstorm relevant context. You may use your knowledge organizer and lecture notes. When time is up, you'll have a chance to compare and add to your list with your table partner. Please begin.

Take a moment to reflect on these moves. Courtney doesn't tell students what to do—she asks them what they need to do. You could read a historical document for many different purposes, and today is no different. By unpacking the prompt, you give students the purpose for reading—and the skills to accompany it.

Core Idea

Unpack the prompt to activate the skill.

In Courtney's class, students are so well-versed in the processes of historical thinking that they name the steps easily. While that won't happen immediately, if you ask students those same prompts before each lesson, they quickly develop competency. Just like knowledge retrieval, skill activation helps students recognize the strategies they already have in their analytical tool chest that will guide their ability to analyze independently.

Michelle De Sousa's 7th-grade students are younger and newer to this process. Watch how she works at even more granular levels to unpack a prompt about the Lincoln-Douglas debates as they prepare for the day's Inquiry Lesson.

WATCH Clip 6: Michelle De Sousa—Activate Skills and Knowledge

Class Discussion—Breaking Down and Contextualizing the Prompt

MICHELLE (TEACHER): Read our prompt for today.

ELIJAH: What role did the Lincoln-Douglas debates play in the American Civil War?

MICHELLE (TEACHER): Take the next minute and a half to annotate the prompt to figure out the historical thinking skill and what we already know about the Lincoln-Douglas debates.

[Michelle monitors student annotation and returns to the front of the room when time is up.]

MICHELLE (TEACHER): Avery, what's our historical thinking skill?

AVERY: Historical causation.

MICHELLE (TEACHER): And what word should we have circled leading to the historical thinking skill?

CHARLIE: We should have circled *role*, and we should have boxed *Lincoln-Douglas debates* and *American Civil War* because these were important words that led to the historical thinking skill.

MICHELLE (TEACHER): Beautifully said. Leah, start giving us some outside evidence. What do we already know about the Lincoln-Douglas debates?

Once you've activated the skill, the power of building knowledge in earlier lessons really starts to bear fruit.

Activate Knowledge

Let's return to Courtney's opening and see what happens next.

Opening Activity

Lesson: Causes of the Stonewall Uprising in 1969

COURTNEY (TEACHER): Okay, considering the question that we are investigating today, what context might we need to fully analyze the evidence from this era? Turn and talk with your table partners. You'll want to reference your lecture notes from Monday and your Unit 9 Knowledge Organizers.

[After 3 minutes of paired work time, the class reconvenes as a whole group. Courtney stands at the whiteboard, marker in hand, ready to write.]

COURTNEY (TEACHER): Okay, so what do we think. What context must we consider?

EMERSON: Well, looking at the year, I would definitely think about the Vietnam War, and particularly the Tet Offensive and the growth of the anti-war protest movement in America.

KENDRA: I'm also thinking about the Civil Rights movement as a whole and using non-violent civil disobedience as a key strategy. During that time, activists made great gains like the Civil Rights Act of 1964 and the Voting Rights Act.

SEAN: Yes, and we can also add the race riots of the late 1960s. The limitations of the Civil Rights movement, particularly in addressing issues facing the Black communities in urban areas like housing discrimination, poverty, and police brutality. There was a wave of race riots in places like Newark. The Kerner Commission cited the racism and discrimination as the root cause of those riots. I wonder if there is a link between that and what happened at Stonewall?

COURTNEY: This is really great. I think that there may be a few other key pieces of context to consider with regards to domestic politics and foreign policy. What else might be happening in America and abroad at this time that might be relevant? Turn to your Unit 9 Knowledge Organizer and discuss with your table partner.

[Students pair off and discuss for 1 minute.]

COURTNEY: What other context might we consider?

LESLIE: I'm thinking about the Cold War in general. We mentioned the Tet Offensive and Vietnam War, but I think it's also important to place this in the larger context of the Cold War and how the containment policy and domino theory forced Johnson's hand in diverting funding away from the Great Society and towards the Vietnam War.

SAM: I can add to that, Leslie. We also know that this had a huge impact on domestic politics because Johnson chose not to run in 1968 and Nixon won that election on a platform of restoring law and order.

[Courtney adds Cold War, Containment Policy, Domino Theory, Great Society, the election of 1968, and Nixon's law and order to the class list.]

Courtney solidified what we learned in Part 2: if you have already taken time to build knowledge, all you need to do is activate it.

> ## Core Idea
>
> If you have already taken time to build knowledge, all you need to do is activate it.

We cannot assume that students will remember to activate the knowledge themselves (because that is the challenge of learning!). Though Courtney prioritizes the activation of knowledge at the beginning of her lesson, not all knowledge is of equal value. Students are prompted to leverage specific resources (Knowledge Organizers, notebooks, and even their peers) to activate the knowledge that is most relevant to the day's lesson. The 10 minutes that Courtney takes to launch her lesson go a long way in teeing up students to succeed.

With both knowledge and skills activated, students are ready to grapple with the evidence. Let's see what happens next.

LET THEM GRAPPLE—GUIDE SENSEMAKING

Courtney leveraged the four SHEG sources to help students think about the causes of the 1969 Stonewall uprising. Here is the list:

Stonewall Lesson Sources

Document 1: Article by Jerry Lisker, *New York Daily News*, July 6, 1969

Document 2: Sylvia Rivera's (a Stonewall participant) speech to the Latino Gay Men of New York in June 2001

Document 3: Dick Leitsch "The Stonewall Riots: The View" from the *Mattachine Society of New York Newsletter*, August 1969 (The Mattachine was a gay rights organization founded in the 1950s.)

Document 4: Article "Gay Power in New York City" published in *The Ladder* (a lesbian magazine) in the Oct.–Nov. 1969 issue.

Monitor Reading and Address the Trend

Courtney gives her students 20 minutes to read the sources and unpack them with four-corner analysis (recall this practice from Part 1: historical context, point of view, audience, and purpose). Let's take a look at what her students do.

Independent Practice—Document Analysis

As students read silently, Courtney walks past the pairs of desks with a clipboard in hand, jotting down what she sees. As Courtney circulates, she notices a similar trend in how students are marking up Document 2, Sylvia Rivera's speech. An example appears here.

Sample Student Four-Corner Annotation of Document

POV
LGBTQ leader

Historical Context
Lavender Scare
homophobia

Document 2

Source: Sylvia Rivera, speech to the Latino Gay Men of New York, June 2001. Reprinted in Centro Journal, Spring 2007. Born and raised in New York City, Sylvia Rivera participated in the Stonewall Riots as a teenager.

Throughout her life, she fought for equal rights for LGBT people. This is an excerpt of a speech she gave at a meeting of the Latino Gay Men of New York, a community organization. We were all involved in different struggles, including myself and many other transgender people. But in these struggles, in the civil rights movement, in the war movement, in the women's movement, we were still outcasts. The only reason they tolerated the transgender community in some of these movements was because we were gung-ho. . . . We had nothing to lose. . . . We were all in the bar, having a good time. Lights flashed on, we knew what was coming; it's a raid. . . . The routine was that the cops get their payoff, they confiscate the liquor . . . a padlock would go on the door. What we did, back then, was disappear to a coffee shop or any place in the neighborhood for fifteen minutes. You come back, the Mafia was there cutting the padlock off, bringing in more liquor, and back to business as usual. . . . The confrontation started outside by throwing change at the police. We started with the pennies, the nickels, the quarters, and the dimes. "Here's your payoff, you pigs!" . . . Once word of mouth got around that the Stonewall had gotten raided, and that there's a confrontation going on, people came from the clubs. But we have to remember one thing: that it was not just the gay community and the street queens that really escalated this riot; it was also the help of the many radical straight men and women that lived in the Village at that time, that knew the struggle of the gay community and the trans community. . . . So then the tactical police force came and heads were being bashed left and right. But what I found very impressive that evening, was that the more that they beat us, the more we went back for. We were determined that evening that we were going to be a liberated, free community.

Audience
New Yorkers

Purpose
Explain the causes of the Stonewall Riots

Stop & Jot

What is limited about the student's annotations of the document? If this is representative of what Courtney is seeing in class, what is the trending error?

_____

_____

_____

_____

What Courtney had anticipated in her planning came true! The students didn't see the key lines to understand that point of view of Sylvia as a Civil Rights movement participant and a transgender advocate.

In one sense, Courtney has done very little up to this point. She has simply walked around the room while students are reading independently and discovered a pattern in their document analysis. Yet that single action makes all the difference. Why? You cannot correct what you do not detect.

Core Idea

You can't correct what you don't detect.

Courtney doesn't wait for class discussion to spot a gap in comprehension. She finds it right away, even before the conversation begins. Courtney wouldn't have seen students' incomplete point of view or historical context if she wasn't looking. And she wouldn't have been able to find these if she hadn't set up systems for her students to make their thinking visible.

Here we see the power of four-corner annotation (described in Part 1): it not only requires students to do historical analysis, it makes it easy for Courtney to spot what is going well and where they struggle. If the four corners frame the meaning, then Courtney's analysis identifies the weak spots in the frame.

Rather than sit on this information, Courtney takes action. Let's see what happens next.

Responding to the Monitoring—Causes of the Stonewall Uprising

COURTNEY (TEACHER): Class, let's pause there for a moment. [Brief pause]. As I'm walking around, I see that you've done an excellent job understanding the significance of Sources 1, 3, and 4, but I'm noticing a limitation in your sourcing of Document 2. Nearly all of you have correctly noted that Sylvia Rivera is an LGBTQ activist, and that homophobia and the Lavender Scare were notable aspects of the time. But what else was happening during this time? Look back at your notes on the historical context of the late 1960s.

[A murmur fills the room as students discuss what they've found in their notes. Courtney drops in on partners to listen, ask follow-up questions, and jot notes on her annotated lesson plan. When the timer chimes, she asks a pair who has identified the missing information to share aloud.]

RYAN: This 1960s was a period of multiple activism movements, like the Civil Rights movement, and Sylvia participated in these, too.

[There is a murmur of agreement.]

COURTNEY (TEACHER):   Good observation. Take a moment to add "civil rights activist" to your POV corner and "Civil Rights movement" to your historical context.

[Students add this to their four corners. Courtney does the same on her projected screen.]

COURTNEY: Let's keep reading. You have about 5 minutes left for sourcing and annotation.

Getting the point of view and historical context right in that moment was critical for students to later be able to hypothesize that Riviera's experience with the tactics of the Civil Rights movement, and the marginalization of transgender people within multiple movements, would have been a compelling new element to the reason why the riots began when they did. Without this more nuanced understanding of the point of view and historical context, the discourse at the start of the chapter would not have been possible.

With a brief, probing prompt, Courtney improved the quality of thinking in the room. Yet Courtney did so not by giving students the analysis, but by activating their knowledge in a strategy that we call *stop the show*. As the name suggests, Courtney stopped instruction at the earliest point of error, in this case overlooked details in the sourcing. Courtney paused student work, named the gap that she saw in annotations, and then redirected students to the resources that would help them close the gap on their own by sourcing and analyzing the curated evidence. After students had the opportunity to improve their own analysis, she brought the class back together to drive home the missing piece of information that would improve the analysis of that given source. A more nuanced understanding of the article's sourcing enabled Courtney students to analyze the text more deeply.

By stopping the show as students read and before they started to form arguments and discuss the question, Courtney ensured that the floor for the quality of student analysis and discourse remained high and that misconceptions and/or surface-level interpretation did not linger unnecessarily long. This early intervention ensures that everyone has a strong entry point into the discussion without reducing the rigor of the work.

Courtney could have taken a similar approach to any struggle she might have found in their writing—one of the corners (i.e., historical context, audience, purpose) or basic miscomprehension of part of the text. In responding to the error in the way she does, she elevates the value of four corners from a simple annotation technique to a teaching tool that reports, in real time, where students are successful and where they struggle. Annotation makes the students' historical thinking visible—and fixable.

> ## Core Idea
>
> Annotation makes historical thinking visible—and fixable.
> Monitoring allows you to respond to what students need.

If you are new to the practices of monitoring and responding, where can you start? Take it one step at a time.

Don't Circulate Aimlessly—Create a Pathway

Brendan Kennedy's 9th-grade World History students are annotating a set of documents as part of their investigation of Aristotle's influence. As they get to work, watch how Brendan moves around the room to review their writing. What does he do while they read?

WATCH Clip 7: Brendan Kennedy—Monitoring

Brendan circulates with purpose.

> ## Core Idea
>
> Circulate with purpose.

He navigates through the desks in a predictable pattern, pausing to read students' early work, jotting notes about what he finds, and offering feedback.

Following is a sketch of the classroom layout. The arrows indicate Brendan's direction of movement, while the numbers reflect student proficiency as based on the results of the most recent assessment. Let's start by taking a look at how students are grouped.

Monitoring Pathway Sample: Brendan's Seating Chart

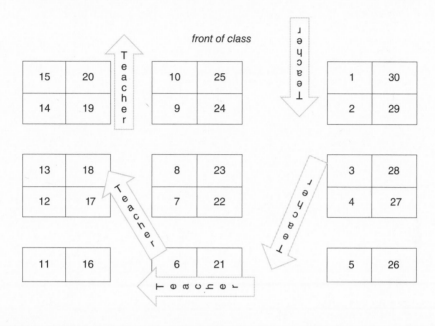

Brendan prefers mixed seating. Notice how students can be paired down the columns with someone of a similar proficiency and across rows with someone of a different proficiency. This is a quick, easy way to differentiate for pair discussions and group work, and students regularly work with others at different levels. Depending on the assignment, students can quickly rearrange the desks to create pairs or quads. And seating is not static. After each round of assessments, Brendan adjusts the seating chart to reflect the newest round of data.

Once work time begins, Brendan checks in on the speedier students; they are more likely to produce something substantive to review in those early minutes. The data he captures here are telling. If these students are in struggle, it typically indicates a larger class-wide struggle. He can stop here and address the whole class before continuing. Once he moves on to students with lower recent proficiency, he collects another set of data unique to that group.

The *U*-shaped classroom follows the same seating principles. As a bonus, it also creates a smaller inner nook where teachers can provide small-group support during independent work time.

Monitoring Pathway Sample: U-Shaped Classroom

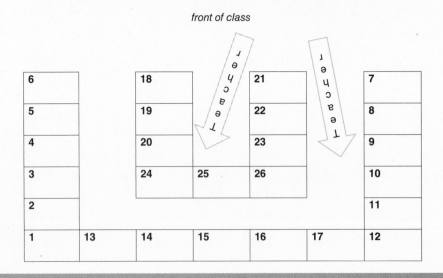

front of class

Creating a pathway to move efficiently around the classroom is the first part of monitoring. Knowing what to look for is the second.

Go Lap by Lap

Take a look at how Courtney applies these monitoring tools to students. How does she signal her priorities to her 8th graders?

 WATCH Clip 8: Courtney Watkins—Name the Lap

Monitoring

COURTNEY (TEACHER): We're going to look at a couple of different sources today, which will ultimately determine do they corroborate our initial hypotheses, or do they challenge them, and if so why? Document 1 on page 2. I'm going to give you 6 minutes. You want to ensure that by the last minute on the timer you're revising or adding on to your hypothesis. I will cue you to move there if you're not yet there with 1 minute left. Six minutes total for Document 1. I'm going to look at your point of view corner first. Make sure you incorporate that person's background and what you're gleaning from the source line about their likely beliefs. Go.

Courtney names what she will be looking for. Before cuing students to start, she stresses that the point of view of this document will be especially important to their analysis. This will be the first element of four corners that she plans to check. If students' annotations are off or limited, it will directly affect the claim they are able to make. Students know that as she monitors in this focused circuit (what we call a *lap*), she will only give feedback about point of view.

Laps maximize instructional impact. Rather than devote the bulk of her feedback to a single or several students' work, Courtney can spread her teaching across the classroom. A singular focus makes it easier for Courtney to provide bite-sized, actionable feedback. Students adjust their learning in real time, and Courtney can see, at a glance, how the class is faring on the task.

Collect Data and Prompt the Error

The beauty of monitoring is that it allows for coaching in-the-minute. Yet it can feel daunting to know what to say to address each individual student's needs. By breaking down the anticipated gaps by the four corners, one can start to use some generalizable prompts to address most scenarios.

Here is a chart of universal prompts that Courtney uses when she finds a trend in the student reading. Each prompt is aligned to the aspect of analysis that is causing the struggle.

Universal Prompts During Document Analysis

Four-Corner	Universal Prompt When Struggling	OR Point Them to a Resource
POV (Point of View)	"What do you know about the author?"	Source line, their previous notes, a knowledge organizer and/or HW reading
HC (Historical Context)	"What's happening at this time?"	Source line, their previous notes, a knowledge organizer, and/or HW reading
AUD (Audience)	"Who was the author writing to?"	Source line
PUR (Purpose)	"Why was this document created?" "Consider the POV, context, and audience—what is it trying to accomplish?"	Source line or other corners
SS (Significance Statement)	"How does this document help you answer the main inquiry for the day?"	Inquiry prompt

By directing students to the source line and classroom resources, Courtney equips them with additional guides to help them resolve blind spots on their own.

Step back and think about the impact of these moves. Before any class discussion has taken place, students have already been primed for sensemaking, and they've strengthened the habits of historical thinking. Each time teachers like Courtney and Brendan monitor and prompt, they accelerate students' growth. By doing so, they also raise the floor for the thinking students can achieve during work time and prepare them to share these thoughts aloud.

CONCLUSION

The past is ripe for investigation. But we don't send students on this journey unprepared. By choosing a worthwhile topic and teaching them how to grapple with the evidence, we set them up as true investigators. By the end of independent work time, students are prepared for the highlight of the class—discourse.

KEY TAKEAWAYS

- When you want them to get it, get them to grapple with evidence.
- The magic of growth lies in productive struggle.
- Don't avoid the struggle. Make it productive.
- Unpack the prompt to activate the skill.
- If you have already taken time to build knowledge, all you need to do is activate it.
- You can't correct what you don't detect.
- Annotation makes historical thinking visible—and fixable. Monitoring allows you to respond to what students need.
- Circulate with purpose.

GRAPPLE WITH EVIDENCE—ONE-PAGER

Activate Knowledge 8–15 min	Knowledge Retrieval
	Do Now (4–6 min):
	• Review spiraled background knowledge or skills needed for today's lesson.
	• Allow independent review of provided key terms using reference sheets and partner quizzing prior to whole group review.
	Class oral review (2–3 min):
	• Briefly review targeted questions based on data collected while monitoring.
	• Lightning quick, hands-down recall of Knowledge Organizer key points.
	• Expect precision in student responses: keep calling on students until you get it.

	Hook (3–5 min)
	Engage students in the lesson: • Frame the lesson as a historical investigation, not as a series of tasks to be completed. • Sell it: model enthusiasm for the content by heightening inflection and vocal/facial expression. • Build a bridge: connect the topic to prior knowledge, an enduring understanding, and/or students' lives.
Activate Skill 6–10 min	Activate Skills (3–5 min)

	Unpack prompt—skill:
	
	• Call on students to read and mark up the inquiry prompt.
	
	• Turn and talk, share out:
	  ○ "In your own words, what is this question asking you to do?"
	  ○ "What's the historical thinking skill embedded in the question?"
	  ○ "Given the historical thinking skill, what would be the best way to set up our graphic organizer?"
	    • (If needed) Model: set up on the board as students set up their own planning pages.
	
	Unpack the prompt—historical context:
	
	• Turn and talk, share out: "What events or developments were happening at this time?"
	
	Activate the skill—document analysis:
	
	• (If needed) Review the four corners annotation strategy (refer to posted reference chart).

Monitor Document Analysis 5–7 min per document, up to 20 min	Monitor
	Send students to work:
	• Remind students of their task and set the timer.
	• Mention your monitoring code: "I'll put a ✓ if your annotations look correct, and I'll circle the four corners annotation if you need to revise."
	Aggressively monitor reading annotations with your monitoring key:
	• Name your laps:
	o "Now I will be looking for your . . ."
	• Lap 1: monitor the most important of the four corners in document 1.
	• Lap 2: monitor the claim annotations and/or significance statement of document 1.
	• Laps 3+: monitor the most important of the four corners and significance statement of each additional document.
	• Remaining laps: monitor the argument/key evidence that they are generating for their thesis.
	Prompt struggling students:
	• Name the error: "You're missing ____." Or "Your context/POV/purpose/audience is off-track."
	• Name what to do: "Go back and re-read __, then __ [paraphrase the source line, ID the speaker, etc.]."
	• Orient students to their resources: "Use your reference sheet to add to your historical context."
	Stop the show: multiple students have wrong answer—foundational conceptual misunderstanding:
	• Name the error: "Several of us are missing a key part of point of view with document 3."
	• Name what to do: "Re-read paragraph ___ and jot a note about WHY the author wrote this. What was her point of view? Revise."

Respond to Data 10–12 min	Close Student Misunderstandings of the Documents
	Respond to the data:
	• Revisit sources where students have confusion or mixed understanding.
	• Use the discourse cycle:
	◦ State a prompt: "What is the significance of document 3? Use your HC and POV to justify your answer."
	◦ Turn and talk.
	◦ Large group share.
	• Facilitate the sharing:
	◦ "Build." "Elaborate." "Agree or disagree?" "Other evidence?" "Other interpretations?"
	◦ Use economy of language (limit teacher talk).
	◦ Chart key arguments and evidence from students.
	• Ensure students take parallel notes.
Launch Inquiry Discourse	**Next Steps**
	See Part 4: Inquiry Lesson One-Pager

SELF-ASSESSMENT

Part 3: Grapple with Evidence	
Set the Stage—Activate What They Need	__/ 5
• Build or activate skill—break down the prompt.	
• Activate needed knowledge.	
Let Them Grapple—Guide Sensemaking	__/ 15
• "Source" the source—student-led four-corner analysis of each document (historical context, point of view, audience, purpose).	
• Monitor student work—create pathway, go lap by lap, collect data and prompt the error.	
Part 3 Score:	__/20

PLANNING FOR ACTION

- Which key ideas from this section resonate the most for you?

- How will you take and/or modify these resources to meet the needs of your class(es)?

_____

_____

_____

_____

_____

_____

Action	Date

Make Sense of It Through Discourse

"Historians ask questions about the past, and they seek evidence that will help answer those questions."

—Keith C. Barton

"The way to right wrongs is to turn the light of truth upon them."

—Ida B. Wells-Barnett

Reconstruction was a seminal moment in US History. In fact, esteemed historian and author of *The Second Founding: How the Civil War and Reconstruction Remade the Constitution*, Eric Foner, considers the Civil War and Reconstruction era in American history to be the second founding of the United States, when the nation was finally forced to confront its original sin of slavery. Foner described this period as a second revolution in American history, when in the aftermath of the Civil War, the passing of the 13th to 15th Amendments and the Reconstruction Act of 1867 (when radical Republicans took over the South) presented the chance to reshape America into a more just and equitable society. The Reconstruction Amendments would go on to serve as the Constitutional basis to fight against threats to civil rights in America. Not only that, it could be argued that the Civil War and Reconstruction era fundamentally expanded the power and function of the federal government as well as Americans' view of it in their lives. However, the economic panic of 1873 and the Compromise of 1877 contributed to the reinstatement of the antebellum racial hierarchy. Particularly in the South, violence and legal maneuvering would pave the way for the Jim Crow era.

In the ever-swinging pendulum of the arc of history, this period has some striking movements in various directions, some of which were seen as revolutionary shifts in nation-building. What better place for students to grapple with history?

For the culminating seminar, Art wants his 11th-grade students to wrestle with the ideas that historians like Eric Foner have raised about this era by considering the following question: To what extent did developments between 1860 and 1877 constitute a social and/or constitutional revolution? After asking students to pose some plausible definitions of revolution (responses: "war," "open rebellion," "new ideas," "precedents," "large-scale change"), Art launches the discourse. We join class just as the conversation begins.

 WATCH Clip 9: Art Worrell—Discourse: On the Nature of Revolution

Sample Class Discussion

Art (Teacher): So, with this foundation [shared ideas about the meaning of revolution], let us begin. To what extent did the developments between 1860 and 1877 constitute a social and/or constitutional revolution?

[After a round of initial responses, one student lands here:]

Kimberly: I think it's a social revolution. He says [Senator John Sherman, a Radical Republican] having a stronger central government will increase patriotism, and due to national pride, ideas that separate America will no longer exist.

[A pause ensues. Rather than insert himself, Art waits for someone in the class to respond.]

Francesca: I'm confused. How is increased nationalism a social revolution, when we've seen high levels of nationalism throughout history? For example, the Era of Good Feelings was a period of strong nationalism, but I wouldn't perceive that as a revolution.

[Classmates contemplate Francesca's critique; Marjorie breaks the silence.]

MARJORIE: I think the revolutionary part that Kim's bringing out is the fact that Americans were starting to value a stronger centralized government over state government. Throughout American history, there were strong feelings toward state governments, which is what caused the South to ultimately secede. So, the fact that Senator Sherman was arguing for a stronger centralized government shows a changing sentiment in American history.

[There is another pause as students absorb Marjorie's words.]

ART (TEACHER): Are there any documents we've missed in answering this question? What else can we argue based on the evidence?

In this simple but important exchange, we see illuminated the magic of strong history classrooms: in the end, with the right knowledge and grappling with evidence, discourse drives depth. And depth makes students into sensemakers of history. All we have to do as teachers is guide them there.

> ## Core Idea
>
> With the right knowledge and evidence, discourse drives depth.
> Depth makes students into sensemakers of history.

Look at the student responses: the talk circulates throughout the room. Students contribute without raising hands, and each can bring thoughts to discourse without being interrupted or dismissed. And they know appropriate ways to disagree, as we see in Marjorie's response. As students drive the conversation, the meaning they make is the fruit of their collaborative labor.

Listening to the substance of students' responses reveals one part of the quality of discourse; the other part is what happens when they aren't speaking. Art does not fill the silence with his words; he gives students time to think. Watch the clip again and note the power of listening. When classmates speak, the others listen attentively. Some watch the speaker, while others take notes or flip back to referenced documents. Art listens quietly as well, waiting for the moment to ask a question rather than dictate the discourse.

What does it take for History class to look and sound like this? A moment like this wasn't fated. It was created—through habits.

GIVE STUDENTS HABITS

One of the high points of media (broadcast, cable, or online) is when individuals engage in authentic, quality discourse. Think of those settings that are most noteworthy for you: some that come to mind for us are Fox Sports NFL broadcasts, Oprah interviews, or PBS Reporters Roundtable. Yet think about how rare those moments are. We all have watched panels of commentators on most news talk shows that are left- or right-leaning. One commentator makes a passionate claim and is pitted against a political opponent that makes the opposite claim (nowhere is this more evident than in formal political debates). These moments are meant to separate one from another, rather than grapple and respond to the evidence of their peer. New counterevidence is often dismissed or at best, minimized, and rarely is it incorporated into a more nuanced argument. Unlike sparring, where the goal of the interaction is for each participant to get better, these conversations play out like a traditional fight where only a single winner prevails.

When people speak with one another with a different goal in mind—understanding—what becomes possible shifts. There is room for new ideas, improved ideas, nuance, and corrections. This isn't ordinary conversation; it's discourse: talk that shapes what and how we think.

Core Idea

Discourse is talk that shapes what and how we think.

The world needs more people talking with—not at—each other. And for students to achieve the dream of becoming inquisitive and engaged citizens, they need ample and deliberate opportunities to embody these skills within the classroom. In a world where this isn't common, developing this capacity means developing new habits: discrete skills that can be chunked, practiced, and internalized over the course of a school year.

Name the Desired Habits

To build habits, it helps to starting by naming them. We first introduced academic habits of discourse in *Great Habits, Great Readers* and then updated them with a lens for grades 5–12 in *Love & Literacy*. They are included here. What do you notice about these moves?

Habits of Discussion 101—Create Conversation		
CORE HABIT	**IDEAL STUDENT ACTIONS**	**TEACHER TALK MOVES**
Project	• Speak audibly and make eye contact with classmates, not just the teacher.	• Put hand to ear or move to opposite side of the room. • "Project" or use a "strong voice." • "Speak to your peers."
Share in turn	• Speak in turn. • Invite others in.	• "Give her a chance to finish her point." • "One voice at a time." • "We haven't heard from everyone yet. Would someone who hasn't spoken yet like a chance?"
Speak as an intellectual	• Use classmates' names. • Use complete sentences. • Address question succinctly.	• "With whom do you agree?" • "Speak in complete sentences." • Point to timer. • "Complete your point and give a peer the floor in 15 secs."
Listen as an intellectual	• Make eye contact with the speaker. • Nod or affirm nonverbally. • Turn to page if speaker references it (pause to give time to turn to page).	• Gesture at students to make eye contact with speaker and/or hands down. • Model appropriate affirmation. • "Destiny, give the class a moment to find the page and confirm that everyone is with you."
Take notes as an intellectual	• Write down/summarize key information. • Evaluate the arguments. • Annotate diagrams.	• Model or select strong student to model strong note-taking. • "If you are not currently participating in the discussion, you should be taking notes." • Provide time at the end for key takeaways to be recorded. • Show call/cold call for a strong summary.

Habits of Discussion 101—Create Conversation		
Build and Critique	**Agree with all or parts of ideas and elaborate:** • "I agree that . . . I would add . . ." • "Mark's point is right, but/and I think there is better/additional evidence for it . . ."	• "Build." • "Agree or disagree?"
	Disagree: • "Actually, there is evidence in the text that refutes that view." • "Respectfully, I have a different view."	• "Agree or disagree?" • "Is there evidence in the text that refutes that view?"
	Examine evidence in a different way: • "I actually viewed that text differently."	• "Is there another way we can view this evidence?"

Habits of Discourse 201—Deepen Discourse		
CORE HABIT	**IDEAL STUDENT ACTIONS**	**TEACHER TALK MOVES**
Activate or Drop Knowledge	• "*X* is . . . ." • "I've heard of *x*. It's . . ."	• "I have some additional context that might be helpful here." • "Some of us are confused by what *x* is, and I was too when I read this. I looked it up, and here's what I found." • "I'd like to give you some formal language for what you just named."
Revoice	• "What you're arguing is *x*." • "If I understand you correctly, then you're saying *x*?" • "Are you saying [paraphrase argument]?"	• "Could you revoice what Dawanna said before adding?" • "If I hear you correctly, you seem to be saying *x*. Is that correct?" • "Are you saying [paraphrase or rework their argument to see if they still defend it]?"

Habits of Discourse 201—Deepen Discourse		
CORE HABIT	**IDEAL STUDENT ACTIONS**	**TEACHER TALK MOVES**
Press for Reasoning	• "Why do you think [rephrase argument]?" • "What evidence supports your argument?" • "How do you know?" • "Could you walk me through your thought process?"	• "Could you explain how you came to that conclusion?" • "What's your evidence?" • "Why/why not?" • "How do you know?"
Problematize	• Name or provoke debate: *"It sounds like we're divided between x and y. I think. . ."* • Name contradictions: "Rene and Gabriel have opposite readings of X. I think . . ." • Play devil's advocate: *"I'm going to play devil's advocate here. I think . . ."*	• Name or provoke the debate: *"Some of you say x. Some of you say y. What do you think?"* • Name contradictions: *"These two ideas are contradictory. How can we make sense of this?"* • Play devil's advocate: *"Allow me to play devil's advocate. I actually think . . ."* or "Who can play devil's advocate?"
Sophisticate	• Zoom in & out: *"I want to focus on x", "X is important because. . . .," "Y creates or makes z in the text."* • Dive deeper into the text: *"Let's turn to page x. Does it support or challenge our theory?"* • Apply within different or new context/perspective: *"What do you think ___ would think about x?* • Give a hypothetical: *"What if . . ."*	• Zoom in: *"What connotations does this diction have?"* • Zoom out: *"So what?" "What's the consequence of that choice?"* • Narrow the focus: *"Given what you've said, what do you make of pages . . .?"* • Feign ignorance: *"I don't understand. I was thinking. . ."* • Apply within different or new context/perspective: *"What would ___ think about this?"* • Give a hypothetical: *"What if . . ."*
Test the Limits	• "I think we have to acknowledge the limitation of this source. . ." • "This source cannot fully answer our prompt because it is lacking. . ."	• Consider the source: *"So in what ways might this source, or these sources, be limited?"*

The habits start off quite simply (being able to be heard) but become progressively more sophisticated. Put together, these academic habits of discussion make intentional, engaged conversation possible. As seen in Art's Reconstruction lesson, students fluidly juggle these moves to keep conversation in motion. And during times when they struggle to do so, the right-hand side of the chart offers prompts that teachers can use to encourage the desired thinking and/or actions.

By the time Art's 11th-grade students filed across the threshold on the first day of school, most already had years of practice using these habits in elementary and middle school. Not all History students are so fortunate. Many of us teach students with far less or limited experience with these habits. Yet Art doesn't take students' abilities for granted. Regardless of their level of mastery, he still devotes time at the start of each year to reinforce these habits, and he models and rolls out new ones as needed to give students the tools they need to keep talk alive. He knows that the habits that make his classroom come to life take deliberate practice and maintenance. As the philosopher Will Durant once wrote in a well-known paraphrase of Aristotle's famous words, "We are what we repeatedly do. Excellence, then, is not an act, but a habit."[1]

Core Idea

We are what we repeatedly do. Excellence, then, is not an act, but a habit.

Let's take a closer look at how you can build and maintain these habits.

Build and Maintain Habits

Revoicing, commonly known as paraphrasing, is a simple but powerful discourse habit. O'Connor and Michaels, who coined the term, explored its multiple functions in pioneering research.[2] Let's consider how Tom introduces students to the concept in AP Seminar. How does he prepare his 11th-grade students to revoice?

 WATCH Clip 10: Tom Brinkerhoff—Model and Roll Out Revoicing

Sample Rollout of a Habit of Discourse—Revoicing

TOM (TEACHER): We are going to learn a new practice for discourse, and it's called *revoicing*. There are three ways that you can authentically revoice something. You could restate what someone's saying in order to build additional evidence. You can restate what someone's saying to form a counterargument. Or you could restate what multiple people are saying in order to come to a common understanding or stamp.

I'm going to model this for you. And . . . scene. Steven Hahn is arguing that the Civil War was caused by slavery. I know that to be true because between 1700–1820, the percentage of African Americans enslaved in the US South rose exponentially. [Pauses.] Think for a second. What type of revoicing did I model?

JOY: This is supporting the argument with additional evidence.

TOM (TEACHER): There are two other ways to revoice: either to challenge the argument with a counterargument or to solidify multiple ideas for a common stamp. Turn to your table group. Let's revoice Hahn's argument in those two ways.

[Students practice for several minutes. Tom calls the class back together.]

TOM (TEACHER): I heard some really good examples of revoicing, and a particularly good one from this table group. Kamara, could you share out your revoice?

KAMARA: I said that, although Steven Hahn is arguing that the Civil War was caused by slavery, others may argue that it was caused by states' rights.

TOM (TEACHER): What type of revoicing did Kamara just show us?

STEPH: I think it's counterargument.

[At the end of the practice session, Tom closes with a reminder.]

TOM (TEACHER): Today in our seminar discussion, we want to think about when we can authentically revoice doing these three things. When you revoice you not only gain a deeper understanding of the content, but you'll push discourse further, and it will allow you to push your analysis further when you do independent writing.

Stop & Jot

How does Tom prepare students to revoice?

_____

_____

_____

Tom doesn't just expect revoicing to happen; he teaches it. Roll out your habits to get discourse rolling.

> ## Core Idea
>
> Roll out your habits to get discourse rolling.

To do so, Tom first provides rationale. Contextualizing new habits within a broader framework of how these behaviors help students grow as thinkers increases engagement and motivation. And young people particularly like to know why they are doing something! Next, he explains what the habit entails. Then he models the skill, briefly, and asks students to discuss what he did. As students share back what they noticed, Tom assesses their level of understanding of the habit. Next, he has them practice the skill in groups, even asking one student to share out a strong example of revoicing. Just as Tom models in the beginning, students revoice to agree, clarify, and name moments of consensus. Last, Tom recaps what students have learned and what he expects to hear in the upcoming discourse.

Tom doesn't simply roll out the habit—he immediately asks students to put it to use in the classroom. The next clip is later on in the same lesson. Students practice revoicing as they discuss scholar Orlando Patterson's theory of social death. Tom's students are using this framework in their comparative study of global slavery. Note how Tom participates in this discussion:

 WATCH Clip 11: Tom Brinkerhoff—Revoicing in Discourse

Sample Class Discussion

MADISON
[reading overarching question]:

To what extent is Orlando Patterson's theory of social death a useful analytic category for describing the condition of marginalization across time and place?

Tom (Teacher):	We want to make sure we're debating both why it's a useful category and why it might be a problematic category, and we're thinking about moments where we might revoice throughout the seminar.
Cameron:	I agree that Orlando Patterson is trying to show the isolation of African Americans in America. By doing that, he is bringing an awareness to society at large—white and black—about the oppression of black individuals in America. That's how I see Patterson's theory of social death being useful.
Tom (Teacher):	What else can we say to build on to the point or change direction?
Avis:	To counter what's been said, I see where you're coming from when you say that the theory of social death is useful because it talks about how African Americans are pushed to the margins of society and they don't have any social connections. But [Patterson's] theory is actually a limitation because we know that Orlando Patterson is a professor and was never a part of this marginalized group. He was always rich and never had to feel the poverty that many African Americans have to go through.
Bakary:	I hear what you're saying in regards to Orlando Patterson not fitting in that African American description, is that what you're saying?
Avis:	Yes.
Bakary:	I kind of agree with that point, but many people argued that Patterson is too centralized on the African American race, and that his theory is flawed because it centralized the viewpoint of African Americans and generalizes their marginalization or oppression.
Curtis:	To build off on the point about how it is too generalized on the African American experience, I think that the social death theory is [limited] because it only begins to understand Blackness in terms of violence and it doesn't begin to understand how Black people can exist in a multitude of ways.

Tom knows that he has one key role to play: prompt the students for the habit when it is not apparent, and let them attempt it, even if imperfectly. As this is students' first attempt at revoicing in discourse, it doesn't sound as smooth as it will by the end of the year. Nevertheless, these early at-bats are important. Why? What students practice becomes what students do. And what students do reflects classroom priorities.

Core Idea

What students practice becomes what students do.

In Tom's class, students continue to practice, refine, and receive feedback on a specific habit until it becomes a natural part of the way they communicate. William James, founder of behavioral psychology, believed that predictable, learned behaviors had the power to unleash the potential of the thinking mind. He argued that the more habitual and automatic we make certain aspects of our lives, the more we can "free our minds to advance to really interesting fields of action."[3] In History class, habits of discussion help students manage the process of discourse, which frees their mind for the rigors of sense-making. (There is also another familiar, cognitive overlap here. As students build robust historical context, they free up the thinking mind to analyze the past, not just recall it.)

Teachers like Tom layer these discourse habits across the school year, moving from simple to more complex as student capacity grows. The goal of this habit-building is to give students the tools they need to engage in an increasingly independent academic exchange of ideas.

Yet even with these habits, quality discourse isn't guaranteed. You need a cycle of teaching—and periodic key teacher moves—to make it happen. Let's see how.

SET THE STAGE FOR DISCOURSE

11th-grade US history teacher Duncan Miller is teaching a lesson from the Stanford History Education Group on the Housing Act of 1949. As part of President Harry Truman's Fair Deal, this act was a part of a larger government initiative to create affordable housing in cities across America. Students are considering the effectiveness of this effort through a five-document case study of post-war Newark, New Jersey.[4]

Let's begin by comparing two different moments of discourse around this topic—one from a limited class discussion (which we will call "Mr. Smith's" classroom) and one from Duncan's actual class. What do you notice are the differences between the two?

Start by reading the following script from Mr. Smith's classroom.

Mr. Smith's Class Discussion— Newark Housing Lesson

MR. SMITH: Ok, so we've had a chance to read and discuss with a partner. What do we think now? Was the development of public housing in Newark after World War II a success? Who wants to go first?

WINSOME: Well, my partner and I both agreed that the development of public housing after WWII was not a success due to the discriminatory practices of the local and federal government.

MR. SMITH: You're referencing the Commission on Civil Rights, I presume? [Nod]. That is a key point of evidence. Please, everyone, write that down. What did the commission find, exactly?

ROWAN: The main issue was the poor maintenance the buildings received, particularly in predominantly Black developments.

MR. SMITH: That's one key point, but don't forget the racial discrimination with assigning tenants. What else can we add to strengthen our argument?

EJ: Because of the history of police brutality, which we know from our notes was a contributing factor to the riots of '66, the police were seen as a threat by the tenants, which is also mentioned in Source 2.

MR. SMITH: Yep, that tracks.

SAUMIK: Yeah, the committee's conclusions in paragraph 6 even stated that the living conditions were oppressive. High-rise projects were designed poorly and created a sense of depression and isolation on the part of the tenants.

MR. SMITH: Absolutely.

TARA: That sounds right to me, too. But it was also the development plan itself. It destroyed the pre-existing community. Document 4 from Michael Immerso, who was a life-long Newark resident, also shows this.

MR. SMITH: This is interesting. So let's synthesize our argument [writes on the board]: Due to the racial discrimination in the assignment, maintenance, and policing of these homes, along with the poor design and placement, public housing in Newark after World War II was a failure. Thumbs up if you agree with this claim. [All but two thumbs, Aisha and Amy, go up.] Excellent. Let's highlight those points as we prepare to write our essays on the topic.

Let's contrast this with Duncan's actual class on the topic. What similarities and differences do you notice between the two conversations?

Duncan's Class Discussion—Newark Housing Lesson

DUNCAN (TEACHER): Okay, so after reading the evidence that we have in front of us, and after your small-group discussions, what do we think now? Was the development of public housing in Newark after World War II a success? Garai, please start us off!

GARAI: Well my partner and I both agreed that the development of public housing after WWII was not a success due to the discriminatory practices of the local and federal government.

[Duncan charts this on the board.]

DUNCAN (TEACHER): Interesting. Courtney, please build.

COURTNEY: This is corroborated by Source 2, the Commission on Civil Rights in 1966, where they investigated discrimination cases in New Jersey. The main issue that stopped the housing developments from being a success was the poor maintenance they received, particularly in the predominantly Black developments.

[Duncan scans the room, nonverbally inviting anyone to speak.]

JAMES: I can build off of that as the Commission notes the racial discrimination in the assignment of tenants to public housing and in the maintenance between Black and White projects. Black projects were not properly cleaned, repairs weren't done quickly, and tenants complained that it was unsafe.

MJ: Yeah and because of the history of police brutality, which we know from our notes was a contributing factor to the riots of '66, the police were seen as a threat by the tenants, which is also mentioned [flips back to handout] in Source 2.

[Several students add to notes, and other students contribute more evidence from Source 2.]

ZULIMAH: Yeah, I agree. It wasn't just the discrimination in the maintenance of these homes, it was the development plan itself. [Taps document] Document 4 from Michael Immerso, a life-long Newark resident, also shows this. The excerpt from his documentary describes how the projects, when built in the First Ward, destroyed the pre-existing community.

DUNCAN (TEACHER): This is interesting. Can someone revoice the argument that is forming?

CADEN: Due to the racial discrimination in the assignment, maintenance, and policing of these homes, along with the poor design and placement of the homes, public housing in Newark after World War II was a failure.

DUNCAN: Thumbs up if you agree with this claim. (All but two thumbs, Pat and Kenneth, go up.) Interesting. Pat, you disagree. What would you say?

PAT: So, should the government have done nothing for low-income Americans at this time? That's what you all seem to be saying. I think we are not considering the progress that was made, although it was less than hoped for.

DUNCAN (TEACHER): Agree or disagree?

Stop & Jot

What similarities and differences do you notice between the two conversations?

_____

_____

_____

Good things are happening in both classrooms. Students refer to historical sources to create and bolster arguments. They use habits of discussion to speak thoughtfully, and in turn. But there's something limiting in Mr. Smith's class: the discourse and the simultaneous sensemaking don't flow as well as they do in Duncan's. Why? Mr. Smith unintentionally blocks it.

Talk bounces between the teacher and a student far more than it does among the students. Mr. Smith speaks after almost every student turn, often determining what students say next by framing the conversation. He also "tips his hand." In his response to Winsome's argument he rounds up the answer by adding more detail and then confirms it himself without letting students evaluate it. And while students are taking turns and citing good evidence, not all voices are being heard—Mr. Smith misses the two students who don't agree with the majority. Instead of hearing the dissenting voices, he moves forward to summarize the conversation.

In contrast, Duncan's participation is more nonverbal than verbal: he charts on the board so that they can see a visual of the evidence being presented and cues students to build on each other's answers. When needed, he prompts students to revoice, and then he identifies the differing perspective and lets it come forward in the class. In doing so, the students do the heavy lifting of argumentation, not the teacher.

Core Idea

Depth in discourse is measured by what students say,
not what teachers synthesize.

Much is lost, collectively, when teacher talk reigns supreme. But much is gained when students dominate the discourse. As teachers, we can transform History class into a space where discourse still lives, and where it has the power to bring the past to life.

So how does a teacher like Duncan make discourse possible? He follows a predictable cycle.

Launch the Discourse Cycle

At the heart of Duncan's history lesson is something we call the *Discourse Cycle*. It is a sequence of moves that can be repeated consistently and incorporates all that we have learned so far. Here's how Duncan implements it.

Everybody Writes

One of the biggest limitations of discourse is that not everyone can actively contribute at once. In large-group discussion, even when students are doing the majority of the talking, each individual student is still participating very infrequently. A turn and talk offers the most participation, and still only 50% of the students can share responses at one time. The risk of discourse is that a few voices can dominate the conversation and give the false impression that everyone is understanding at the same level as those who share publicly. This is what often leads us as teachers to misread the comprehension of the class. We confuse visible action (head nods, facial expressions, or raised hands) with invisible thinking.

However, if we start a class with a short writing prompt (or evidence analysis), we make thinking visible for all of our students. That's why Duncan always asks his students to write independently before discourse begins. It's his first chance to see what every student thinks.

During Everybody Writes, students can break down and contextualize the given prompt. They read the source or sources for significance, annotate the four corners, and mark up key lines. (We covered this in detail in Parts 1 and 3.) By the end of this independent work time, each student has drafted an original independent response, and Duncan knows where the conversation will begin. All he has to do is look at what they write. Writing, like annotation, makes historical thinking visible. To see what they think, read what they write.

> ## Core Idea
>
> Don't confuse visible action (head nods, facial expressions) with invisible thinking. To see what they think, read what they write.

Writing is also a process of distillation. As students rummage through what they know (schema, evidence, and skill), they begin to impose their own understanding on the events of the past. As they write, these fledgling thoughts and arguments are put to the test, with students reshaping both into defensible claims. Doug Lemov calls this work *formative writing*, as it captures in-progress thinking rather than summative writing, which reflects an established, more finalized argument.[5] The more opportunities students have for formative writing, the more thoroughly they can develop and hone their own thinking. Structures like Everybody Writes give students consistent opportunities to practice historical thinking in a low-stakes environment. Acclaimed essayist Joan Didion once wrote, "I don't know what I think until I write it down."[6] The same holds true for students of history.

Having everyone write first also strengthens the discourse by adding intellectual preparation. A student who might otherwise be reluctant to share will feel much more comfortable when they have already gathered their thoughts. Moreover, students who need time to process before they share are now equipped to share as readily as those who are more likely to respond immediately. You've leveled the playing field for participation in the class.

While independent writing marks students' first crack at concretizing what they think, it won't be the last. The next step sharpens it further.

Peer-to-Peer Discourse

After reviewing written responses, Duncan cues students to discuss what they wrote with a partner. A low murmur fills the room. Duncan moves between the pairs to listen, clipboard in hand.

Peer-to-peer discourse gives students a smooth on-ramp to large group discourse. Many students, especially those who are less likely to speak in class, find that sharing first with a peer prepares them to share more comfortably during whole-group discourse. This is also students' first chance to improve the quality of their argument by listening to someone else's. They can revise what they've written to include evidence or counterevidence they've learned from listening to a partner. Just as Everybody Writes offers every student the chance to show what they know, peer-to-peer discourse ensures that every student gets the chance to speak and be heard before whole-group conversation.

Having worked out many of the kinks in small groups, students are ready to take their thinking to the big stage.

A Note on Being Responsive to Student Needs

Some students may need a little help to get started on a topic at hand before tackling the blank page of Everybody Writes. For those students, inserting a turn and talk before writing (rather than after) can be a quick adjustment to generate the writing. Be mindful about peers just repeating their peers' thoughts, which is why we recommend using this option intermittently.

Facilitate Large-Group Discourse

Let's return to Duncan's discourse. This time, we've included only his words and actions. What do you notice?

Duncan's Class Discussion, Take 2: Newark Housing Lesson

DUNCAN (TEACHER):   Okay, so after reading the evidence that we have in front of us, and after your small-group discussions, what do we think now? Was the development of public housing in Newark after World War II a success? Garai, please start us off!

[Duncan charts this on the board.]

DUNCAN (TEACHER):   Interesting. Courtney, please build.

[Duncan scans the room, nonverbally invites anyone to speak.]

DUNCAN (TEACHER):   This is interesting. Can someone revoice the argument that is forming?

DUNCAN (TEACHER):   Thumbs up if you agree with this claim. [All but two thumbs, Pat and Jordan, go up.] Interesting. Pat, you disagree. What would you say?

DUNCAN (TEACHER):   Agree or disagree?

Stop & Jot

What are the key moves Duncan makes (and doesn't make) to facilitate discourse?

_____

_____

_____

Duncan does not add a single piece of content, but he shapes the room with his actions (and inactions). Let's break down those actions.

Maximize Student Talk

Duncan makes an intentional choice at the start of discourse. Unlike Mr. Smith, he quickly steps back. This move signals that students are to talk mostly to each other, not to him. While teacher-led instruction is effective in Build Knowledge lectures, it becomes a hindrance in Inquiry Lessons. Students need space to think and speak, which they can't do if we're taking up all the air space. To maximize student talk, Duncan minimizes his own.

Core Idea

To maximize student talk, minimize your own.

This is seemingly simple but can be one of the hardest things to do in the moment. You have so much knowledge that you want to share! Many of the teachers we highlighted in the book remark about having to "bite their tongue" to keep from talking automatically—it needs to be an intentional, conscious decision.

Strategically Call Students

For his next move, Duncan calls on a specific student to launch discourse—Garai. A review of the clipboard that he carried around during the Everybody Writes shows why. Here are his notes. Why do you think he chooses a student like Garai to start the conversation?

Duncan's Clipboard—Newark Housing Lesson

Prompt: Was the development of public housing in Newark after WWII a success?

Anticipated Response	Students Who Have Each Response
An Exemplar response	
While public housing in Newark did have some successes in offering affordable housing to people in need, ultimately it was failure because the housing was poorly maintained, policies were discriminatory and racist, and it disrupted existing neighborhoods.	Pat
Evidence of Success:	
• Public housing to Newark did expand access to quality housing, at least early on.	
• In the first two decades of public housing efforts in Newark dilapidated buildings were demolished, substandard plumbing was updated, and more low-rent housing was made available (D1).	Pat
• Affordable housing given to WWII vets.	
Evidence of Failure:	
• Residents complained of racial discrimination in assigning residents to housing, high rents, and poorly managed facilities (D2, D3).	Garai, Carlos
• Many cited the terrible living conditions inside public housing. As a further insult to residents, existing communities were rarely consulted on urban planning, which resulted in historic neighborhoods being dismantled (D4).	Courtney, James
• Families, neighbors, and businesses were ripped apart to make way for the construction of public housing (D4).	Caden, Zulimah

Before Duncan walked around, he knew what he was looking for. As discussed in Part 1, Duncan had already created an exemplar response as a part of the lesson preparation process. As he prepped for discourse, Duncan drafted the key evidence that needed to be part of the conversation and a plausible, defensible thesis that recognized both sides of the argument. So while he walked around, he noted what students were able to do. Knowing what you're looking for allows you to look for what students know.

Core Idea

Know what you're looking for to look for what they know.

Jotting down which students have which answers is a great starting place for discourse, because it allows Duncan to make sure all perspectives come to the surface—and to push them when there is a gap. To understand why this is so important, let's consider his other options.

Imagine that Duncan started by cold calling a student who happened to have a near exemplar response (like Pat). That student shares out to a flurry of nods. Other students pick up the argument and restate various portions of it throughout the conversation. Duncan smiles, confident that students are grappling with the meatiest parts of the prompt. Yet the exit tickets say otherwise, with most students writing responses similar to their Everybody Writes responses. What went wrong? Students didn't work together to forge new meaning. They retold the cognitive work done by single student. For learning to happen, build the house of discourse from its foundation.

Core Idea

For learning to happen, build the house of discourse from its foundation.

Calling on a student like Garai who has one part of the answer makes generative discourse more likely. It establishes a baseline that most students can access, and it encourages students to add additional information that hasn't been mentioned. Starting with a strong response just limits the conversation for everyone else and doesn't allow the teacher to see what they can generate together. Duncan waits to call on a stronger student response until the class is stuck and needs it. When he does, he uses universal prompts.

Leverage Universal Prompts

If you watch Duncan teach over time, you will notice the simplicity he brings to discourse by relying on a set of prompts that he doesn't have to think about. They appear in the following table. Think about how each prompt keeps the dialogue in motion without taking over.

Universal Prompts for Discourse

Press for Reasoning
• Why/why not?
• "Prove it/evidence"
• "So what?"

Open Up the Debate
• "Build"
• "Elaborate"
• "Agree/disagree"

Revoice
• "If I hear you correctly, you seem to be saying x. Is that correct?"
• "Are you really saying [paraphrase argument to see if they still defend it]?"

To Encourage More Voices
• "I would love to hear what ____ thinks about this."
• "Let's hear from a few more voices to get more perspectives."
• "We need to share the airtime here."

Press for Reasoning prompts ask students to justify their answer with additional evidence, which includes key terms and vocabulary. Open Up Debate prompts do just that: encouraging students to flesh out answers or inviting others to co-construct the argument. And you saw the power of revoicing in the earlier clips from Tom's class.

These succinct words or phrases tell students exactly what they need to do to enrich discourse. While these prompts start in the hands of teachers like Duncan, students will quickly follow that lead and make them their own. And discourse stays on track without Duncan using significant airtime to manage it.

A Note on Using Prompts to Keep Discourse Evidenced

It can be easy for teachers to fall into a trap of letting an early idea dominate the discourse when stepping back, or have students rely strongly on opinion or less-substantiated arguments, which could allow misconceptions to circulate. The following strategies give students a greater ability to manage on-topic discourse when maximizing student talk.

Puncture Groupthink: When the class latches on to an early idea, puncture groupthink by playing devil's advocate, introducing new evidence or directing students to a piece of contradictory evidence, or by sending students back to the evidence with a pointed question to push or challenge their thinking.

Require Evidence: Never let claims live without supporting evidence. Consistently reinforce the use of sources throughout discourse to ground arguments.

Leverage the Room: Strategically call on students based on monitoring data to clarify arguments or add contrasting analysis.

Effective prompting maximizes the potential for generative discussion. Charting captures it.

Chart Discourse

To help student thinking during the discourse, and the quality of their notes at the end, Duncan charts the main points of evidence on a T-chart as they are mentioned. As students share sourcing and evidence, he jots contributions into the relevant category. Duncan chose this organizer because it efficiently allows students to consider the program's continuum of possibilities (from successful to unsuccessful). It appears next.

Charting Discourse—Newark Housing Lesson

Housing was a success	Housing was not a success
Docs. Do Now, 1	**Docs. 2, 3, 4**
• More low-rent federally funded housing available in Newark • Dilapidated housing demolished • Affordable housing for veterans who returned from WWII	• Facilities poorly maintained • Unsafe and unsanitary conditions • Discriminatory housing practices • Rent strikes by tenants **OE (Outside Evidence)** • Most high-rise housing torn down in the 1990s

Note how easy this charting is when Duncan has already prepared what he is looking for during Everybody Writes—it is the same evidence!

The value of charting discourse—and not just hearing it—is another way to make thinking visible. While visual learners find charting especially helpful, all students benefit from being able to see their understanding captured as it evolves. In addition to supporting in-progress thinking and collaborative sensemaking, it's also a handy way for teachers to monitor student engagement and participation. Following discourse, teachers like Duncan often post these charts in high-visibility areas, like the front of the room, so that students can independently reinforce their own learning.

So far the moves we've discussed help students prepare and share what they think during discourse when they are on track. In this next section, we'll dig into what History teachers can do when students need a nudge to go deeper.

Deepen Discourse

For many of us, discourse in a dream scenario sounds a particular way, namely, a fluid, generative stream of talk. There are few pauses, backtracks, or moments of confusion. But this vision of discourse doesn't reflect the rugged realities of sensemaking. Forging meaning is a messy process, and that is naturally reflected in the way that discourse sounds. Conversation may burst, dip, or even stall out at points—that is part of the process. The past is not simple. Neither is thinking or talking about it.

When conversation dips or stalls out, landing on limited or incorrect analysis, teachers can make a few strategic moves to make the struggle productive and help students to continue sensemaking.[7]

Drop Knowledge

Scott's 9th-grade AP History students are examining the reasons why the 1892 Homestead Strike, which pitted underpaid iron workers against wealthy factory management, turned violent. But first, they need to know the major players and their motivations. Here's how Scott makes sure they have the information they need in this Stanford History Education Group–adapted lesson.[8]

 WATCH Clip 12: Scott Kern—Drop Knowledge

Drop Knowledge Sample Class Discussion Homestead Strike

Scott: I want to give you a definition of a term we've heard a bunch, but we haven't covered explicitly yet . . . this group called the Pinkerton Detectives. This was a private security force of guards and detectives that businesses would hire to try to break up strikes. They would keep workers out of factories, they would try to intimidate them, and they would often use violence in pursuit of that [goal].

Have this information in your mind as you analyze the outcomes of the Homestead Strike.

In just a few seconds, Scott did what we call dropping knowledge. By defining the Pinkerton Detectives, Scott gives students valuable historical context to analyze the actors and outcomes of the Homestead Strike. Without a shared understanding of particular terms, especially those that are directly relevant to the analysis at hand, students can be hindered in their sensemaking.

The act of dropping knowledge builds on the cognitive premises we discussed in Part 2: Build Knowledge. Without sufficient knowledge, deeper analysis can be unreachable. Scott drops knowledge when there is a moment in the lesson when students can get no further (whether by schema or thinking) on their own. Scott uses it sparingly, but when he does, it has a powerful effect on discourse. He drops knowledge to bridge the gap from limited to deeper analysis.

> ## Core Idea
> Drop knowledge to bridge the gap from limited to deeper analysis.

Although Scott drops knowledge by defining a term, teachers can also drop knowledge by sharing relevant historical context, for example, "At this time, x was also happening," and naming key actors, for example, "James was a Radical Republican." Whatever you choose to share, know that the purpose of dropping knowledge is to further what students can do on their own. The right knowledge at the right time is a powerful tool.

> ## Core Idea
> The right knowledge, at the right time, is a powerful tool.

Let's visit Art's class to see another way to deepen discourse—with sophistication.

Sophisticate

Art's 9th-graders are learning about the Progressive Era (1896–1916), a period of reform when activists called for the large-scale rehaul of various industries and asked for government intervention to protect workers' rights, break up trusts, and prevent industry monopolies. In this Inquiry Lesson, students are analyzing the extent to which the Progressive Era was successful. Most students settle on a fairly simplistic analysis— that the Progressive Era wasn't as successful as it could be because it didn't fully address the needs of African Americans. Then Art intervenes with two questions. What value do they add to discourse?

 WATCH Clip 13: Art Worrell—Sophisticate Discourse

Sophisticate Discourse Sample Class Discussion—
The Progressive Era

[You can watch the full discussion in the video clip. Here are Art's two prompts.]

Art: Why wasn't that [the challenges of African Americans] front and center?
Art: Who were the Progressives?

   With these simple questions, Art asks them to consider why? The students were pressed to go further into contextualization and the point of view of the critical players of this time period—skills that will be replicable for all of historical analysis. Prompts that sophisticate are about enriching limited arguments.

Core Idea

Prompts that sophisticate are about enriching limited arguments.

   Another way to do this is to problematize.

Problematize

Let's return to Art's Reconstruction lesson that we observed in the opening. Pay close attention to Francesca. What impact does her contribution have on the discourse?

WATCH Clip 14: Art Worrell—Problematizing in Discourse

Sample Class Discussion

Art (Teacher): So with this foundation [shared ideas about the meaning of revolution], let us begin. To what extent did the developments between 1860 and 1877 constitute a social and/or constitutional revolution? Shatavia, do you want to kick us off?

[After a round of initial responses, one student lands here.]

KIMBERLY: I think it's a social revolution. He says [Senator John Sherman, a Radical Republican] having a stronger central government will increase patriotism, and with national pride, ideas that separate America will no longer exist.

[A pause ensues.]

FRANCESCA: I'm confused. How is increased nationalism a social revolution, when we've seen high levels of nationalism throughout history? For example, the Era of Good Feelings was a period of strong nationalism, but I wouldn't perceive that as a revolution.

[A brief pause ensues, as classmates contemplate Francesca's critique. Marjorie breaks the silence.]

MARJORIE: I think the revolutionary part that she's bringing out is the fact that they're starting to value a stronger centralized government over state government. Throughout American history, there were strong feelings toward state governments, which is what caused the South to ultimately secede. So the fact that he's arguing for a stronger centralized government shows a new idea in American history.

Francesca problematizes the conversation with a counterargument. She pushes back against Kimberly's assertion by using the example of the Era of Good Feelings as an example of increased nationalism that didn't lead to revolution.

> ### Core Idea
> Problematize the conversation with a counterargument.

Similar to sophistication, problematizing directly addresses the complexity of studying and thinking about the past. It helps puncture groupthink (coalescing around a single argument) and invigorates debate. Doing so makes the art of history sensemaking come alive.

Test The Limitations

Let's return to Art's Reconstruction lesson. Art attempts to push the thinking of his students in yet another way before he closes out the discussion.

Evaluating the Source

Lesson: The Legacy of Reconstruction

ART (TEACHER): Wow, we have built out some very compelling arguments about the extent to which there was a true social or Constitutional revolution in America between 1860 and 1870. As we prepare to wrap up our conversation and stamp a few key ideas, I'd like you to consider one other question. Having examined this curated list of sources, how might they be limited? Take a few moments to review the documents again with this question in mind. Okay, please turn and talk with your partner.

[Students flip through the documents as they turn to discuss with their partner. Art circulates to listen in on conversations.]

LONDON: I'm thinking about the Constitutional side of this question. I'd love to hear from an attorney or from the Supreme Court at the time. Wouldn't they be the best voices to tell us about how revolutionary any of the Reconstruction amendments were at that time?

ART (TEACHER): Interesting. Let's build on that.

JALISSA: Well we do know a little about how the Supreme Court viewed the 14th amendment at the time. The Supreme Court's ruling in the Slaughterhouse cases, which I think was 1873, really limited the impact of the 14th Amendment.

ART (TEACHER): How?

JALISSA: Well the Slaughterhouse cases established the precedent that individual states could limit the protection of the privileges and immunities clause of the 14th Amendment. It pretty much opened the door to *Plessy v. Ferguson* and legal segregation.

KELLY: Yeah, this set is definitely limited without a look at the important cases that centered on the 14th Amendment at that time. I'd even love to hear from someone like Homer Plessy. Despite the important step of getting Constitutional Amendments like the 14th Amendment, it would be some time before those amendments effectively worked in favor of Black Americans like they were originally supposed to.

ART (TEACHER): That's fascinating. One way to think about the limitations of a document or any evidence that we have, is to consider what part of the story is intentionally, or unintentionally not accounted for. You all are doing a really nice job of that now. How else might this evidence be limited?

One of the most important skills that we can help our students develop is the ability to evaluate the quality of various sources of information. In a time when our students are constantly bombarded with information from a range of sources, they must be able to recognize and account for bias, find corroborating evidence, and consider the limitations of the sources that they do have so that they know what new information they need to seek out. This work goes beyond merely pointing out the weaknesses of the source. Instead, it requires students to consider at what point does a given source(s) cease to be of value to us as historians? What part of the story can we *not* tell from this document? What does the author leave out and why? What is intentionally or unintentionally not addressed? This is the essential work of a historian and a civically engaged member of society.

CONCLUSION

Understanding the past takes work. At the beginning of the process, students are simply observers of a multifaceted debate shaped by past and current historians. But by the end of it, they have entered the arena themselves as fellow historians, and they've felt the thrill of sparring and honing their analysis. All that's left for them is to solidify what they've learned.

KEY TAKEAWAYS

- With the right knowledge and evidence, discourse drives depth. Depth makes students into sensemakers of history.
- Discourse is talk that shapes what and how we think.
- We are what we repeatedly do. Excellence, then, is not an act, but a habit.
- Roll out your habits to get discourse rolling.
- What students practice becomes what students do.
- Depth in discourse is measured by what students say, not what teachers synthesize.
- Don't confuse visible action (head nods, facial expressions) with invisible thinking. To see what they think, read what they write.
- To maximize student talk, minimize your own.
- Know what you're looking for to look for what they know.
- For learning to happen, build the house of discourse from its foundation.
- Drop knowledge to bridge the gap from limited to deeper analysis.
- The right knowledge, at the right time, is a powerful tool.
- Prompts that sophisticate are about enriching limited arguments.
- Problematize the conversation with a counterargument.

INQUIRY LESSON ONE-PAGER

Activate Knowledge (if needed) 8–15 min	Activate Skills and Knowledge (3–5 min)
	Review notes:
	• Review notes from the grappling with evidence: four-corner annotations, significance statements, and preliminary thesis. Call on students to read and mark up the Inquiry prompt.
	Recall the unpacking of the prompt:
	• Turn and talk, share out:
	○ "In your own words, what is this question asking you to do?"
	○ "What's the historical thinking skill embedded in the question?"
Guide Discourse 10–12 min	**Evaluate Arguments**
	Repeat the discourse cycle:
	• Start with the prompt and initial student hypothesis:
	○ "Based on the evidence, why did Lincoln issue the Emancipation Proclamation in 1863?"
	• Everybody Writes (if not already done)
	• Peer-to-peer discourse (turn and talk or small-group discussion)
	• Large-group discourse
	Facilitate the large-group discourse:
	• Strategically call on students:
	○ Start with students who have more limited arguments.
	• Maximize student talk:
	○ Volleyball, not ping pong: call on two or three students before responding.
	○ Use universal prompts:
	• "Build." "Elaborate." "Agree or disagree?"
	• "How can you prove/corroborate this?" "Where do you find evidence for this?" "Other evidence?"
	• "Are there other interpretations?"
	• Chart key arguments and evidence from students:
	○ Ensure students take parallel notes.
	Deepen the discourse:
	• Drop knowledge:
	○ "We seem to have a lack of knowledge of this historical figure. She is _____. How does that deepen your analysis?"
	• Sophisticate:
	○ "Use [key information/terms/events] to enhance your response."
	○ "Why then and there?"

	• Problematize:
	○ "How can you critique this interpretation?"
	○ "No one has cited this opposing source in their argument. How do you reconcile this voice with your argument?"
	○ "Hmm. You cannot explain a change with a continuity. So what is the change? Go back to your sources."
	○ "If I interpreted your argument broadly, you seem to be saying that we would have been better off with no action at all. Is that true? If not, how would you revise your argument?"
	• Test the Limitations (evaluate quality):
	○ Consider the source: So in what ways might this source, or these sources, be limited?
Revise & Stamp 3 min	**Lock in the Learning**
	Revise your claim:
	• "With these new understandings, go back and revise your claim and solidify/revise the evidence you will use."
	Stamp the takeaways—argumentation and metacognition:
	• Turn and talk on arguments: "What new understanding have we established about ___?" "How did your thinking about ___ change in this lesson?"
	• Go meta: "What skills did you use today to enhance your analysis and argument? What do you want to remember to do next time?"

SELF-ASSESSMENT

Part 4: Make Sense of It Through Discourse	
Give Students Habits • Roll out desired habits of discourse: model, debrief, and practice. • Reinforce habits of discourse through the year: prompt students to use them.	__/ 5
Launch the Discourse Cycle • Begin every discussion with a brief Everybody Writes. • Follow this with peer-to-peer discourse (e.g., turn and talk, small groups, etc.).	__/ 5
Facilitate Large-Group Discourse • Chart discourse to capture student thinking. • Minimize teacher talk. • Strategically call on students, leverage universal prompts, and chart discourse. • Deepen discourse: drop knowledge, sophisticate, problematize, and/or test the limitations.	__/ 10
Part 4 Score:	____/20

PLANNING FOR ACTION

- Which key ideas from this section resonate the most for you?

- How will you take and/or modify these resources to meet the needs of your class(es)?

_____

_____

_____

_____

_____

_____

Action	Date

Stamp and Measure the Learning

"Who controls the past controls the future: who controls the present controls the past."

—George Orwell

"Know from whence you came. If you know whence you came, there is really no limit to where you can go."

—James Baldwin

On September 9, 1739, in the British colony of South Carolina, an Angolan-born man named Jemmy (also known as Cato) led a band of enslaved people down the road. They walked carrying banners emblazoned with the word "Liberty!" and chanted the same. More enslaved people joined the group as they swept through the area. By the time they set up camp near the Edisto River, drumming and dancing, their numbers had swelled to almost 100.

Daybreak, however, would tell a much different story.

The Stono Rebellion (also called *Cato's Conspiracy* or *Cato's Rebellion*) was the largest rebellion of enslaved people in the Southern colonies. It was also the deadliest: the quelled revolt ended with the deaths of 25 colonists and 35 to 50 Africans.[1]

In Dan Balmert's 11th-grade Inquiry Lesson, students are discussing why the Stono Rebellion unfolded in South Carolina in 1739. (This, as you remember, is a 4QM Question 3 inquiry that asks, "Why then and there?") Students already have historical context of slavery in the Southern colonies and they know what makes South Carolina's system unique. Dan built strategic schema about the demographics of the colony's majority-Black population (primary enslaved, African-born, from rice-growing regions), as well as common methods of resistance.[2] Refusal to work, slowing down work, breaking tools, and even poisoning enslavers were all strategies carefully employed by enslaved peoples to fight back against slavery. Open-armed rebellion, like that of Stono, was less commonly attempted. Rebellions of that type often ended in the mass executions of enslaved Blacks and even harsher laws governing the lives of survivors.[3]

Nevertheless, in South Carolina in 1739, an enslaved Black man named Jemmy (Cato) and his followers chose this method. Why did the Stono Rebellion, as it came to be called, take place in 1739 in South Carolina? Why then and there?

During that lesson's discourse, students have named three or four plausible explanations. Watch what happens near the end of the lesson.

Sample Class Discussion

DAN (TEACHER): Let's pause our discussion here. [Pauses.] Can I have a few volunteers restate the claims we've heard today about the causes of the Stono Rebellion?

[After a few moments of silence to think, students begin to share out without raising hands.]

MICHAEL: Enslaved people in South Carolina had more autonomy than enslaved people in other areas because planters lived off-site, and the task system granted them free time after finishing the day's responsibilities. That gave them more time to plan and execute the rebellion.

JAMIE: That's true, but it's also really important that South Carolina's majority-Black population was "re-Africanized" after the arrival of a large influx of African-born people that worked the rice and indigo plantations. Some, like Cato, were said to be literate, and that literacy served as a base for their leadership.

SCHUBERT: Honestly, I think one of the biggest factors was Spain's decision to offer freedom to enslaved Africans in English colonies if they could reach Spanish territory. Florida wasn't too far from South Carolina.

DAN (TEACHER): Thanks, everyone. So we've heard a few different directions where we could go with our thinking today. Take what you've heard here, go back to your notes, and revise what you have written. Based on the historical context we've built and the sources we used, why did the Stono Rebellion happen in 1739? Synthesize your response using two or more possible pieces of evidence shared today.

Rather than just moving forward, Dan takes a moment to synthesize all the plausible arguments presented during the lesson. Why? The learning isn't ready to fly until you put a stamp on it.

Core Idea

The learning isn't ready to fly until you put a stamp on it.

When you have participated in a rich discourse, you have learned a lot, but it is also likely that you cannot remember everything that has been discussed. By taking a few moments to stamp the key takeaways, Dan gives his students a chance to write down the key arguments, internalize them, and get ready to use them to improve their writing. Without the stamp, the rich discourse won't translate as effectively into the quality of the writing or the synthesis of the learning.

What is striking about Dan's class is that he didn't provide that stamp: the students did, and in their own words. Here is how Dan does it.

STAMP IN STUDENT VOICE

In Part 4, we discussed the power of revoicing—keeping ideas in motion. Stamping is a final use of revoicing.

The simple part is calling on students to answer. The harder part is listening well for the key arguments as they manifest in discourse. Dan was ready for this. He knew the documents and was familiar with many of the potential arguments. By internalizing the lesson beforehand, Dan freed up space in his mind to evaluate claims in the moment.

> ## Core Idea
>
> Learn the lesson to free your mind to listen.

From there, he could quickly discern when a student was arguing something that was historically defensible, even if different and something that was off and historically indefensible.

Yet hearing ideas shared in class is not enough. To make the learning linger long past the bell, students have to put the big ideas in their own words. Don't just hear it, say it.

As students verbalize the big ideas of the inquiry, they exercise intellectual muscles that would go unused if the teacher recapped the major points or if this step was skipped entirely. Just as Everybody Writes helps students produce formative thoughts at the start of class, stamping records both formative and summative ones at the end. We stamp the learning to make it stick.

> ## Core Idea
>
> Don't just hear it: say it and write it.
> Stamp the learning to make it stick.

Stamping doesn't just work for high school students; it is equally effective (and arguably even more important) in middle school. Let's return to Courtney's class to see what this looks like.

Courtney's 8th-grade students are deep in a study of American society during the 1920s. In this lesson, they are focusing on how this time period affected the lives of American women. The topic of the day's inquiry is whether the 1920s represented an era of liberation for women. These final minutes of discourse show where students have landed.

 WATCH Clip 15: Courtney Watkins—Stamp in Student Voice

Sample Class Discussion

COURTNEY (TEACHER): So were the 20s a period of liberation for women? And how has your thinking changed? Talk to your partner first. Go.

ERIC TO PARTNER: The 20s [were] not a period of liberation for women because despite the superficial changes, traditionally their roles were the same.

[After the pair-share ends, Courtney calls the whole class together.]

COURTNEY (TEACHER): [Were] the 20s a period of liberation for women?

JUSTIN: The 1920s [were and weren't] a time of liberation for women. We see that women got more opportunities in the 1920s in a way, dress more [differently] and jobs they could have, but they were still oppressed by society. Society was still having them follow traditional values like marriage.

CHINARA: At first, I thought the 20s [were] a point of just positive changes. Reading the documents, I realized that there were still people that disagreed with the movement. There were also people like Nellie Ross [first woman governor of Wyoming—Source 1] [who] agreed with the movement but also wanted women to be respectful [of] the old views.

LIAM: After reading the documents, I will say it goes both ways because we can see that women gained some freedom based on their clothes and jobs, but there were still other people like Black women [who] didn't get freedom. If you're talking about women, you have to talk about all women. So once you say that, if a portion of women are not getting freedom, but this portion is, then it's not really equal.

Discourse isn't done until it's stamped: not just saying it, but writing it.

STAMP IN WRITING

Writing is a key component of history instruction. From activating knowledge in the opening Do Now (Part 2) to writing your preliminary understanding of a source (Part 3—Grapple with Evidence) or your initial thesis (Part 4—Everybody Writes), writing helps students shape and examine their understanding as it develops. This is also true at the end of a lesson. Dan carves out time at the end of every lesson for students to write down their stamps. Through the iterative process of daily writing, student arguments grow more nuanced, thorough, and historically defensible.

While it's difficult to quantify how much more we remember when we write versus passive listening, multiple studies have confirmed that writing enhances memory. Education researchers Mueller and Oppenheim theorize that writing encourages more cognitive work than other recording methods because it requires students to actively work with the information as they pick it apart to summarize its most important elements.[4]

Revise Your Final Claim

After giving students time to rework their original claim, Dan cues students to turn and talk. Sharing these stamps with a peer exposes them to alternative, historically defensible claims. From this exchange, students can revise their own stamps to reflect the more nuanced, multifaceted thinking anticipated in a final argument. We revise to finalize.

Core Idea

Revise to finalize.

Following is an original claim written by a student before discourse and a revised claim written after. Note the difference.

The Power of the Stamp—Sample Student Work

Prompt: Why did the Stono Rebellion occur in South Carolina in 1739?

	Written Response
Orlando Before (Everybody Writes)	The Stono Rebellion was the result of the use of the task system in South Carolina, which offered enslaved people more freedom and autonomy than other places in the British Colonies.
Orlando After (Stamp)	The Stono Rebellion occurred in the context of a not yet codified slave system in low country South Carolina, where proximity to Spanish territory and the possibility of escape were ever present. Enslaved people showed knowledge of this context and a willingness to exploit it when possible. It was in this context that leaders like Jemmy (who had been taught to read and write) were willing to take the huge risk of rebellion in order to free not just themselves but others. As we read in the Nash piece, "The intensity of slave revolt was in direct proportion to the opportunity slaves had." The South Carolina low country of 1793 presented just such an opportunity.

Orlando strengthens an existing argument to make it more sophisticated. For all students, whether they're on track or offtrack, revision enhances learning.

Unlike the earlier formative writing that students did, this stamp represents multiple days of thinking and writing about Stono. Doug Lemov notes that we often ask students to produce summative writing early in instruction before they've had a chance to fully grapple with the complexities of what we've asked them to consider. Spacing out and delaying summative writing until later in the unit gives students more time to develop something substantive to say,[5] as does receiving student and teacher feedback on formative writing.

STAMP THE THINKING (GO META)

Upon completion of the unit and final stamp, Dan encourages students to turn the focus inward. Part of the essential work of a historian is understanding how you arrived at the argument. To encourage development of this skill, Dan periodically asks students to reflect and write about their own process.

Dan caps the Stono Rebellion lesson with the following metacognitive question.

Go Meta Final Reflection—Stono Rebellion

What steps did you take to arrive at your final argument? What thinking did you do to allow you to come that conclusion?

This is what Cori has to say.

Go Meta Final Reflection—Stono Rebellion Student Response

This process highlights how historians read sources differently from how I have been thinking I should read them. I almost never took exactly what a source said to help me answer my question, because the sources themselves were very limited by their origin and purpose. However, I dug around for clues and especially clues that I saw repeated (corroboration) and then used those to help inform my overall argument. While all three sources had limitations, I ultimately got an idea for my final arguments from something that I saw reoccurring in all three, despite them having such vastly different agendas.

The one piece of evidence that was corroborated in all three sources was the fact that enslaved people had knowledge of their proximity to Spanish Florida and the Spanish proclamation offering freedom to enslaved runaways from British territories. By the end, I walked away with the idea that this was the most important factor in providing the conditions in which an individual like Jemmy would be motivated to act.

Two people benefit from Cori's response: Cori and Dan. From Cori's perspective, this reflective exercise allows her to name the steps of her thinking, breaking down a complex set of skills and knowledge into a bite-sized, systematic process. Dan also benefits, as reading Cori's response shows him what Cori is able to name about her own development, which could indicate opportunities for additional enrichment or remediation of certain skills.

In Part 1, we referenced historian Sam Wineburg, who described historical thinking as an unnatural, yet essential act. By ending the unit with a metacognitive reflection, the unnatural becomes namable and thus more replicable. If students can break down the process into steps, they can use these steps in other contexts.

APPLY IT—ASSESS

A week after the Stono lesson described in the opening, Dan assigns students the following. What do you notice about it?

Sample Task Assessment

Read the accompanying documents. Then answer the following prompt.

DBQ task: Explain the causes of the development of the institution of slavery in the period from 1607 to 1750.

In your response, you will be assessed on the following:

- Respond to the prompt with a historically defensible thesis or claim that establishes a line of reasoning.
- Describe a broader historical context relevant to the prompt.
- Support an argument in response to the prompt using all but one of the documents.
- Use two additional pieces of specific historical evidence (beyond that found in the documents) relevant to an argument about the prompt.
- For at least two documents, explain how or why the document's point of view, purpose, historical situation, and/or audience is relevant to an argument.
- Use evidence to corroborate, qualify, or modify an argument that addresses the prompt.

This task assessment is not about the Stono Rebellion, and it shouldn't be—they have already discussed that in class. Rather, the task assesses the same historical thinking in a different context. By doing so, Dan can see what students can do on their own—without prompting, discourse, or other classroom scaffolds. Assessments are one of the best ways to capture students' most authentic, independent thinking.

Core Idea

Assess with new content to evaluate students' independent thinking.

Here's how to make them as useful as possible.

Choose a New Setting, but Already Contextualized

Slavery is not a new topic for Dan's students; they've come across it in previous units. But they never examined it from this inquiry perspective. While it might be tempting to give students a radically new and unfamiliar context to test their thinking, it also takes away something vital that they need for their analysis—historical context. As we've said before, students need something (background knowledge) to think about in order to form arguments. The best way for Dan to measure students' historical thinking skills is to see them applied in a different, yet familiar context. Lean on their previous knowledge of the historical context, but force them to apply it to a new scenario.

Align to the Rigor of Year-end Assessments—and Do So in Multiple Ways

As presented in *Driven by Data 2.0*, standards are meaningless until we define how to assess them. And any good assessment will combine multiple forms to achieve the best measure of mastery.[6] Multiple-choice tests, open-ended questions, long-form essays and performance-based assessments are a few of the most well-known ways for History teachers to measure learning. The keys to full mastery are to give students at-bats in those many different forms, ensuring they align to the rigor of the year-end assessment.

For example, if students can do the assessment without analyzing a new historical source, they are not applying the full range of skills needed to make sense of history. Similarly, if they are only asked basic recall questions and don't need to assess historical context, they are simply being assessed on their ability to memorize information.

Regardless of the structure or length, a strong assessment typically includes the following (as part or all of the assessment).

Characteristics of a Strong Task Assessment

- An inquiry question aligned to one or more of the 4QM thinking skills
- A source or sources unfamiliar to students that they have to read and analyze
- A topic (historical development or event) about which students can gather the necessary knowledge from the sources themselves or from their previous learnings in class
- A reading and writing component
- A rubric/scoring method that aligns to the rigor of year-end assessments

---

(If you are looking for a quick resource to help, the Stanford History Education Group offers free Beyond the Bubble History Assessments. These document-based tasks use Library of Congress digitized sources to measure specific historical thinking skills.)

Dan regularly assesses students, not solely to track their learning over time, but to show him where his teaching has been most and least effective. The information he gains here informs his future instruction, showing him what to reteach, where to enrich, and how to monitor his class in real time (see Part 3: Monitor Reading for a reminder of how assessment data can inform in-class teaching).

Much more can be said and has been written about assessment—if you want a more in-depth review, *Driven by Data 2.0* is a good place to start.

CONCLUSION

As History teachers, we want the work that we do to live on in our students. With the right amount of practice of unpacking compelling prompts, drawing sufficient historical context, and analyzing diverse sources, students are prepared to craft arguments and plumb the complexities of the past.

You now have nearly all the pieces you need to help your students make history. To help put this all together, Part 6 offers a final, comprehensive implementation rubric as well as two units (one from US History and one from World History) with samples of each type of lesson plan for each topic. Through a series of connected and scripted Build Knowledge, Grapple with Evidence, and Inquiry Lesson plans, you will see how it all fits together.

KEY TAKEAWAYS

- The learning isn't ready to fly until you stamp it.
- Learn the lesson to free your mind to listen.
- Don't just hear it, say it and write it. Stamp the learning to make it stick.
- Revise to finalize.
- Assess with new content to evaluate students' independent thinking.

SELF-ASSESSMENT

Part 5: Stamp and Measure the Learning	
Stamp in Student Voice • Students verbalize the biggest takeaways in their own words.	__/ 5
Stamp in Writing • Students record their stamps in writing and revise final claims.	__/ 5
Stamp the Thinking (Go Meta) • Students reflect on their own thinking to build metacognition.	__/ 5
Apply It—Assess • Choose a new setting that is already contextualized for the students. • Align to the rigor of year-end assessments.	__/ 5
Part 5 Score:	__/ 20

PLANNING FOR ACTION

- Which key ideas from this section resonate the most for you?

- How will you take and/or modify these resources to meet the needs of your class(es)?

_____

_____

_____

_____

_____

_____

Action	Date

Part **6**

Put It All Together

> *"Nations reel and stagger on their way; they make hideous mistakes; they commit frightful wrongs; they do great and beautiful things. And shall we not best guide humanity by telling the truth about all this, so far as the truth is ascertainable?"*
>
> —W.E.B. Du Bois

You now have all the pieces of effective History instruction. We have taken the self-assessment checks at the end of each part and merged them into a comprehensive implementation rubric. The power of this rubric lies in its ability to illuminate teaching. By detailing what is most important in effective History instruction, the implementation rubric provides a roadmap that guides lesson planning, teaching, and assessment.

IMPLEMENTATION RUBRIC—MAKE HISTORY

Part 1: Define the Destination	Score
Choose the sources: • Offer multiple perspectives of a historical actor, event, or development (e.g., dominant and overlooked voices, left- and right-leaning, etc.). • Make the sources manageable for the time that you have (one-page source per class period, or four paragraph-long sources).	__/ 10
Design the prompt and exemplar response: • Prompt is clear and specific (4QM), compelling (relevant and thought-provoking), multifaceted (multiple possible answers), and manageable (doable in the time allotted). • Prompt addresses a key historical thinking skill. • Exemplar response sets the bar for what students should do to meet the task's demand. • Know-show chart names the knowledge and skills students need for the task.	__/ 10
Part 2: Build Knowledge	
Activate knowledge: • Do Nows, class oral reviews, and resources (e.g., knowledge organizers)	__/ 10
Frontload knowledge: • Hook them and make the story memorable. • Build note-taking habits. • Have a clear check-for-understanding activity (e.g., four-sentence summary, six-panel storyboard, etc.).	__/ 10
Part 3: Grapple with Evidence	
Set the stage—activate what they need: • Activate skill—break down the prompt. • Activate needed knowledge.	__/ 5
Let them grapple—guide sensemaking: • "Source" the source—student-led four-corner analysis of each document (historical context, point of view, audience, purpose). • Monitor student work—create pathway, go lap by lap, collect data, and prompt the error.	__/ 15

Part 4: Make Sense of It Through Discourse	
Give students habits: • Roll out desired habits of discourse: model, debrief, and practice. • Reinforce habits of discourse through the year: prompt students to use them.	__/ 5
Launch the discourse cycle: • Begin every discussion with a brief Everybody Writes. • Follow this with peer-to-peer discourse (e.g., turn and talk, small groups, etc.).	__/ 5
Facilitate large-group discourse: • Chart discourse to capture student thinking. • Minimize teacher talk. • Strategically call on students, leverage universal prompts, and chart discourse. • Deepen discourse: drop knowledge, sophisticate, problematize, and/or test the limits	__/ 10
Part 5: Stamp and Measure the Learning	
Stamp in student voice: • Students verbalize the biggest takeaways in their own words.	__/ 5
Stamp in writing: • Students record their stamps in writing and revise final claims.	__/ 5
Stamp the thinking (go meta): • Students reflect on their own thinking to build metacognition.	__/ 5
Apply it—assess: • Choose a new setting that is already contextualized for the students. • Align to the rigor of year-end assessments.	__/ 5
Total Rubric Score:	____/100

To help illuminate this process from start to finish, we have included four sets of lessons:

- Reconstruction (HS AP US History)
- Westernization or Southernization (HS AP World History)
- Pre-Columbian North America (6th-grade)
- Westward Expansion (8th-grade)

The Reconstruction and Westernization lessons are presented here in Part 6, and all four sets are available and print-ready in the online materials.

SAMPLE LESSON PLANS—RECONSTRUCTION (AP US HISTORY)

Reconstruction (featured in Part 4) was a watershed moment in US history and a core part of any survey of American history. The changes wrought during that time—from the 13th to 15th amendments, to the Reconstruction Act of 1867, to the Black Codes and Compromise of 1877—reflected a nation caught between opposing groups that proposed strikingly different visions of a reunited union.

These lesson plan materials come from Amir Ballard's high school classroom. Note the three lesson types—Build Knowledge, Grapple with Evidence, and Inquiry—that are woven throughout the unit. The Build Knowledge lessons that launch the unit provide students with a story from the end of the Civil War to the end of Reconstruction. By front-loading this knowledge in Lessons 1 & 2, Amir frees himself and his students to dive deeper as they wrestle with interesting and diverse evidence. The subsequent lessons enable students to grapple with powerful questions that challenge or add nuance to the story told in the initial Build Knowledge lessons. How did newly freed African Americans in the South define their freedom in the aftermath of the Civil War? Who or what killed Reconstruction? What should be the legacy of Reconstruction? These questions drive the unit, which culminates in an assessment designed to measure their growth as historical thinkers.

UNIT 5 PACING CALENDAR

Week 1					
Cycle Topic (Content): Reconstruction					
• **Cycle Essential Question: To what extent was Reconstruction successful by 1877?**					
				Thursday, 11/18	**Friday, 11/19**
[Finish Previous Unit]				**Lesson 1** **LP Type:** Build Knowledge **Topic:** Civil War **SWBAT:** • Compare the Union and Confederate preparedness and strategies during the war. • Describe the reasons for the Union victory in the war. • Create a set of detailed Cornell Notes from a lecture.	**Lesson 2** **LP Type:** Build Knowledge **Topic:** Reconstruction **SWBAT:** • Describe the effects of Reconstruction. • Evaluate the extent to which Reconstruction changed America. • Create a set of detailed Cornell Notes from a lecture.

Week 2				
Cycle Topic (Content): Reconstruction				
• **Cycle Essential Question**: **To what extent was Reconstruction successful by 1877?**				
Monday, 11/22	**Tuesday, 11/23**	**Wednesday, 11/24**	**Thursday, 11/25**	**Friday, 11/26**
Lesson 3 **LP Type:** Grapple with Evidence and Inquiry **Topic:** Defining Freedom **SWBAT:** • Analyze and explain how the formerly enslaved defined their freedom by reading *Letter from Jourdon Anderson: A Freedman Writes His Former Master.* • Explain how a source provides information about the broader historical setting within which it was created.	**Lesson 4** **LP Type:** Grapple with Evidence and Inquiry **Topic:** The Propaganda of History **SWBAT:** • Trace the historiography of Reconstruction. • Analyze and explain W.E.B. DuBois's central claim in an excerpt from "The Propaganda of History." • Explain how a source provides information about the broader historical setting within which it was created.	**Thanksgiving Break No School**		

Week 3				
Cycle Topic (Content): Reconstruction				
• **Cycle Essential Question: To what extent was Reconstruction successful by 1877?**				
Key vocabulary:				
Monday, 11/29	**Tuesday, 11/30**	**Wednesday, 12/1**	**Thursday, 12/2**	**Friday, 12/3**
Lesson 5 **LP Type:** Grapple with Evidence and Inquiry **Topic:** Who killed Reconstruction? **SWBAT:** • Analyze the reasons for the end of Reconstruction in America. • Establish a line of reasoning in response to a prompt by addressing *both* sides of an argument.	**Lesson 6** **LP Type:** Grapple with Evidence **Topic:** Plessy v Ferguson **SWBAT:** • Analyze the justification for the *Plessy v. Ferguson* decision. • Explain how a source provides information about the broader historical setting within which it was created.	**Lesson 7** **LP Type:** Inquiry Seminar **Topic:** Reconstruction **SWBAT:** • Evaluate the extent to which Reconstruction was successful by 1877. • Explain how a source provides information about the broader historical setting within which it was created.	**Lesson 8** **LP Type:** Guided Practice **Topic:** Reconstruction **SWBAT:** • Source and corroborate a given primary source document within a body paragraph of an essay.	**Lesson 9** **LP Type:** Assessment **Topic:** Reconstruction **SWBAT:** • Write a document-based essay on the legacy of Reconstruction. (Prompt: Evaluate the extent to which Reconstruction was successful by 1877.)

What follows are a few of the lessons to give you a feel for how they fit together:

Build Knowledge Lesson

Build Knowledge Lesson	
Teacher: Ballard	Date:
Course: Advanced Placement US History	**Unit Title:** Unit 5: Reconstructing America, 1861–1877

Objective	
Skills/Content: *By the end of today's lesson, what will students know and be able to do?* • Describe the effects of Reconstruction • Evaluate the extent to which Reconstruction changed America	**Assessment:** *How will students demonstrate mastery of the objective?* By. . . Writing a paragraph essay in response to a prompt

Unit-ending assessment:

Long Essay Question (taken from AP US History Test):

Some historians have argued that the American Civil War and Reconstruction periods constituted a second American Revolution. Support, modify, or refute this contention using specific evidence.

	Identify the Knowledge Students Need
Prepare	**Key Conceptual Understandings:** *What key ideas do students need to take away from today's lesson?* • Lincoln's assassination drastically altered the political landscape in America in 1865. Andrew Johnson, a southern Democrat, repeatedly opposed efforts to punish Southern states and enact legislation to bring about racial equality in America. • Radical Republicans in Congress stood in opposition to Johnson. They were able to use their majorities in both houses of Congress to frequently overturn presidential vetoes and pass legislation and enact government programs focused on civil rights and racial equality. • The Constitution was amended to guarantee equal protection under the law (14th Amendment) and voting rights for all males (15th Amendment). • Republican gains were limited as Democrats slowly regained control of the South. They enacted laws to deny suffrage to Blacks, support white supremacy, and legalize segregation. By the end of the 19th century, although Constitutional and legislative progress had been made on racial equality, little had changed for Blacks living in the South.

Activate Knowledge 5–15 min	**Launch the Class**
	Do Now: **Directions:** Answer the following questions about Reconstruction based on your knowledge of the events of the Civil War. 1. Based on what you know about the US immediately before the Civil War, and the effects of the war itself, what should be the priorities of Reconstruction? Why? *Students might say: racial equality for newly freed Black Americans, reparations/economic stimulus, rebuilding the destroyed parts of the North and South.* 2. What would have to happen in order for the Reconstruction period to be considered a success? Why?
Hook 2–5 min	**Tell a Memorable Story**
	Hook: "Today we're going to begin our unit on the Reconstruction Era. It's hard to imagine what was facing America after the Civil War without seeing it, so here are a few images of the nation at this time." Project the following slides:  Source: The Library of Congress / Public Domain Fredericksburg, VA

Source: U.S. National Archives and Records Administration (NARA) / Wikimedia Commons / Public Domain
Charleston, SC

Source: The Library of Congress / Public Domain
Atlanta, GA

"And when the war ended and the 13th Amendment took full effect, this is what the 1860 census said about the population of the South."

Project this slide:

Number	States	Free Population	Slave Population	Total	Percentage of Slaves
1	South Carolina	301,271	402,541	703,812	57.2
2	Mississippi	354,699	436,696	791,395	55.2
3	Louisiana	376,913	332,520	709,433	46.9
4	Alabama	529,164	435,132	964,296	45.1
5	Florida	78,686	61,753	140,439	44.0
6	Georgia	595,097	462,230	1,057,327	43.7
7	North Carolina	661,586	331,081	992,667	33.3
8	Virginia	1,105,196	490,887	1,596,083	30.8
9	Texas	420,651	180,388	601,039	30.0
10	Arkansas	324,323	111,104	435,427	25.5
11	Tennessee	834,063	275,784	1,109,847	24.8
12	Kentucky	930,223	225,490	1,155,713	19.5
13	Maryland	599,846	87,188	687,034	12.7
14	Missouri	1,058,352	114,965	1,173,317	9.8
15	Delaware	110,420	1,798	112,218	1.6
		8, 280,490	3,949,557	12,230,047	32

Almost 4 million enslaved people were now free.

"Considering these images and this chart, what was the nation facing when the Civil War ended in 1865? Turn and talk with your partners."

Take two or three responses.

Tell the Story:

Tell the Story
10–20 min

"One question as the war came to an end was how to readmit Southern states to the Union. The Constitution did not address this, so Lincoln had a lenient plan called the 10% plan, which allowed readmittance if states took an oath and abolished slavery as stated in the 13th Amendment. This previewed Lincoln's desire for unity and peace after the war. But Congress had different plans. The Republicans who controlled Congress had gained the nickname 'Radical Republicans' for what many Americans considered extreme views on racial equality and Reconstruction. Their leader was Thaddeus Stevens, a Congressman from Pennsylvania who was an unapologetic supporter of abolition and equality for the freed people the South. Stevens and the Radical Republicans wanted to punish the South for the war so they put forth their own plan for Reconstruction called the Wade-Davis Bill—a stricter substitute for Lincoln's plan and an indication that Congress would not turn Reconstruction over to the President."

[Continue the story. Additional topics covered: Readmitting the States, Death of a Vision, Congress vs. President]

*Stop & Jot

After the final slide, pause and have students review and compare their notes and respond to the following question in their notebooks:

• What were the effects of Reconstruction on freed people in the South?

Preliminary Check for Understanding in Small Groups (then chart the answers)

What were Lincoln's goals in Reconstruction?

- 10% plan: Lincoln wanted to allow the Southern states to rejoin the union as efficiently as possible; his conciliatory tone in the 2nd inaugural makes clear that he wants to heal the nation after the war; Lincoln's support of the 13th amendment makes clear that he is unwilling to compromise on slavery.

What were Johnson's goals?

- Johnson also wants to bring Southern states back into the fold, but he wants to punish Southern leaders first; he's also unconcerned with equality for Blacks and as a Southerner and enslaver does not believe in racial equality.

What were the Radical Republicans' goals?

- Radical Republicans want to aggressively punish Southern states for the war and make it difficult to rejoin the Union, grant full equality for Blacks, and amend the Constitution to make these changes permanent.

Continue the Story:

Early in Reconstruction, African Americans were elected to Congress for the first time ever; Republicans immediately gained control of most Southern states. African Americans' time in power is short-lived as southern Democrats retake control of most state governments; KKK and other hate groups form to disenfranchise Blacks in the South; removal of federal troops and lack of support from Johnson hastens these problems.

Slavery was ended through the 13th amendment and Blacks were given Constitutional equality through the 14th Amendment; hate groups formed to prevent them from receiving these benefits; Black Codes were enacted to target Blacks and prevent them from achieving equality in Southern society. Despite early successes, Blacks make up a permanent underclass in Southern society; legislation addressing their disenfranchisement and lower social status isn't passed for 100 years.

Southern society moved to sharecropping in the wake of the Civil War; this put many Southern Blacks in permanent debt to white landowners and essentially reinforced the economic hierarchy that was in place before the war.

Check for Understanding 15–20 min	Check for Understanding

Check for Understanding:

Peer-to-peer:

- Team up students to review notes with each other and fill in gaps.

Class oral review:

- Ask key questions to check for their understanding of the lecture.
- Chart for reference.

Exit Ticket:

Did Reconstruction change America?

- Answers will vary.
- Students may say that compared to the era leading up to it, Reconstruction resulted in significant gains for African Americans, especially in the South. Immediately after the war, Republicans in Congress were able to push for near equality in many respects, build schools and roads, amend the Constitution (over the objections of obstructionist Andrew Johnson), and use the military to enforce rule of law in the South.
- Students may also say that Reconstruction ultimately failed to deliver on the promise of equality that many hoped for. Although Radical Republicans were able to make some immediate improvements in American society and infrastructure, ultimately those gains were short-lived. The Southern Democrats reorganized and consolidated their power after the war.

Grapple with Evidence and Inquiry Lessons

This lesson plan starts with Grappling with Evidence and then moves into Inquiry. Depending on the length of your class periods, you may find yourself splitting a lesson plan like this into two: one class period for grappling with evidence and the following class period for inquiry.

Grapple with Evidence Lesson	
Teacher: Ballard	Date:
Course: Advanced Placement US History	**Unit Title:** Unit 5: Reconstructing America, 1861–1877
Objective	
Skills/Content: *By the end of today's lesson, what will students know and be able to do?* • Analyze the reasons for the end of Reconstruction in America • Establish a line of reasoning in response to a prompt by addressing BOTH sides	**Assessment:** *How will students demonstrate mastery of the objective?* By. . . • Writing an analytical thesis statement with a clear line of reasoning with multiple sub-claims

Key Conceptual Understandings: *What key ideas do students need to take away from today's lesson?*

- (From HW reading) The Compromise of 1877 handed Republican candidate Rutherford Hayes the presidency in exchange for withdrawing the last federal troops from the South. This effectively left it up to states to enforce Reconstruction legislation and policies.

- The Panic of 1873 and economic scandals of the Grant administration shook the nation economically and diverted attention from civil rights. Support for Reconstruction in the North waned as Americans focused on solving economic and political problems and lingering racism continued to cause some Northerners to withhold support.

- The rise of the KKK and White League in the South systematically denied African Americans rights that were supposed to be guaranteed by the Constitution and Reconstruction laws. They used terrorism* and intimidation to restore white supremacy across the South. (* Terrorism is the unlawful use of violence and intimidation, especially against civilians, in the pursuit of political aims, according to the *Oxford Dictionary*.)

Unit-Ending Assessment:

Long Essay Question (taken from AP US History materials)

Some historians have argued that the American Civil War and Reconstruction periods constituted a second American Revolution. Support, modify, or refute this contention using specific evidence.

Question(s)	Who or what ultimately ended Reconstruction?
Source(s)	• Albion Tourgee, Letter on Ku Klux Klan Activities, *New York Tribune*, August 1870 • Abram Colby, testimony to a joint House and Senate Committee in 1872 • Thomas Nast political cartoons: August 5, 1865 and March 14, 1874 • Heather Cox Richardson, *The Death of Reconstruction: Race, Labor and Politics in the Post–Civil War North, 1865–1901*, Harvard University Press, 2001
Activate Knowledge 5–15 min recommended	**Activate foundational knowledge** **Do Now:** 1. **What was the Compromise of 1877? Why is it often cited as the formal ending of Reconstruction in America?** Rutherford B. Hayes was given disputed electoral votes to win the Election of 1876 by Southern Democrats in exchange for removing federal troops from the South. Without federal enforcement, Reconstruction legislation and policies relied on state and local governments for support. 2. **List and describe some of the successes of Reconstruction:** Reconstruction Amendments, Civil Rights Act, election of Black senators and congressmen, building of schools throughout the South.

Hook:

TW say, "We've spent several days now exploring Reconstruction in America after the Civil War. In particular, we've seen that the laws and policies put forth by Republicans were very radical for their time—they called for full equality for African Americans in the South. However, as you probably know, Reconstruction didn't last. In fact, many historians consider 1877 the end because of the deal made to elect Rutherford Hayes as you read in your HW reading. Let's get a sense of what was really happening on the ground for people in the South during Reconstruction. To do that, we'll look at a famous political cartoon. It was published in the *Tuscaloosa Independent Monitor* in September of 1868.

*Project the slide below on the overhead for students

Source: Quadell / Wikimedia Commons / Public Domain

Under an article reads, "The above cut represents the fate in store for those great pests of Southern society—the carpet-bagger and scalawag—if found in Dixie's land after the break of day on the 4th of March next."

TW say, "Turn and talk with your partner for 30 seconds: What does this image and article indicate about Reconstruction in Southern states like Alabama?"

TW call on two or three students for responses. If not mentioned, stamp:

  – Southerners view Reconstruction as something to be stopped

  – KKK growing in strength

  – Reconstruction policies will be difficult to enforce/enact

TW say, "Today we're going to explore why Reconstruction ended. You'll be presented with evidence that may support what we just looked at together, but also new evidence that supports alternative reasons. In the end, you'll need to synthesize them all to determine what or who ultimately is to blame for ending Reconstruction."

Set up the task: (2 min)

TW cold call a student to read the task aloud to the class:

Who killed Reconstruction—the North or the South? **(Historical thinking skill: Causation)**

SW take 90 seconds to brainstorm prior knowledge they already have that could help answer the question. They should use their notes and HW reading.

Prior Knowledge: Compromise of 1877, Radical Republicans, Reconstruction Amendments, KKK, Southern Democrats, Grant Administration, Panic of 1873

TW say, "You have 15 minutes to read the first two sources. Annotate them with your four corners and start to prepare your initial argument."

| Monitor and Discourse on Document Analysis
15 min recommended | **Identify the trends and prompt to improve student work** |
| | **Monitoring Lap 1—Exemplar Annotation (Four Corners)** |

*The documents should be analyzed by students independently in sets of two. First have students analyze Documents 1 and 2 (both indicating reasons that the South ended Reconstruction) and then lead discourse over both documents. Once that has been stamped, have students analyze Documents 3 and 4 (both indicating reasons that the North ended Reconstruction) and then lead discourse over both documents. Once that has been stamped, move to the summative discourse which considers the whole set in response to the prompt.

Document 1

Source: Albion Tourgee, Letter on Ku Klux Klan Activities, *New York Tribune*, August 1870

Note: Tourgee was a white, Northern soldier who settled in North Carolina after the war. He served as a judge during Reconstruction and wrote this letter to the North Carolina Republican Senator, Joseph Carter Abbott.

It is my mournful duty to inform you that our friend John. W. Stephens, State Senator from Caswell, is dead. He was foully murdered by the Ku Klux in the Grand Jury room of the Court House on Saturday . . . He was stabbed five or six times, and then hanged on a hook in the Grand Jury Room . . . Another brave, honest Republican citizen has met his fate at the hands of these fiends . . .

. . . I have very little doubt that I shall be one of the next victims . . . I say to you plainly that any member of Congress who, especially from the South, does not support, advocate, and urge immediate active and thorough measures to put an end to these outrages . . . is a coward, a traitor, or a fool.

FOUR-CORNER ANNOTATION:

(POV = point of view; HC = historical context; PUR = author's purpose; AUD = intended audience; SS = significance statement):

POV: Carpetbagger, soldier, judge

HC: 15th Amendment, first AA in Congress

PUR: Criticize Congress for failing to stop KKK activities in the South.

AUD: Abbott

SS: The KKK terrorized and threatened anyone trying to help enforce Reconstruction efforts in the South.

Since: Tourgee was a Republican judge in the South; he was likely to be targeted by the KKK as they sought to undermine efforts to protect civil rights.

Document 2

Source: Abram Colby, testimony to a joint House and Senate committee in 1872.

Note: Colby was a formerly enslaved man who was elected to the Georgia State Legislature during Reconstruction.

Colby: On the 29th of October 1869, [the Klansmen] broke my door open, took me out of bed, took me to the woods and whipped me three hours or more and left me for dead. They said to me, "Do you think you will ever vote another damned Radical ticket?" I said, "If there was an election tomorrow, I would vote the Radical ticket." They set in and whipped me a thousand licks more, with sticks and straps that had buckles on the ends of them.

Question: What is the character of those men who were engaged in whipping you?

Colby: Some are first-class men in our town. One is a lawyer, one a doctor, and some are farmers . . .They said I had voted for Grant and had carried the Negroes against them. About two days before they whipped me they offered me $5,000 to go with them and said they would pay me $2,500 in cash if I would let another man go to the legislature in my place. I told them that I would not do it if they would give me all the county was worth . . . No man can make a free speech in my county. I do not believe it can be done anywhere in Georgia.

FOUR-CORNER ANNOTATION:

POV: Formerly enslaved, GA state Congress

HC: Election of 1872, KKK Act

PUR: Describe efforts of KKK to suppress AA suffrage and political power in the South.

AUD: Congress

SS: The KKK used violence to intimidate.

Since: This happened after the North won the Civil War and passed legislation protecting Black Americans in the South; it's surprising that Southern communities were openly violent.

DISCOURSE CYCLE (Peer-to-Peer, Then Large Group)

What arguments are these two sources making about what ended Reconstruction?

[Questions to ask if students are struggling to unpack certain key information:]

According to Tourgee, what kinds of people are being attacked by the KKK? Why are these people being targeted?

- *The KKK was attacking government officials and judges. Both groups had the power to pass laws hurting the KKK and to try members of the KKK. Thus they were seen as prime threats and targets.*

How does the account in Document 1 support the idea that the KKK was a terrorist organization?

- *Stephens was killed in a gruesome way that would be widely talked about and potentially send a message to others. The fact that he was killed in a court also indicates that all aspects of the judicial system were being attacked and that there was no safe place for supporters of civil rights.*

Why did the KKK attack Colby according to Document 2?

- *Colby was a Black leader in the South who threatened white control. He was attacked because he refused to abdicate his political power to the KKK and Southern whites.*

What types of people made up the KKK group that attacked him? What does this indicate about the KKK in the South at that time?

- *The KKK was composed of professionals like doctors and lawyers—people who were well respected in the community. This indicates that the KKK had become intertwined and normalized in Southern society. Being a member of that group was not out of the ordinary for anyone of any position in a community.*

MONITOR ROUND 2—DOCUMENTS 3 AND 4

Document 3

Source: Two political cartoons from artist Thomas Nast. The first was published on August 5, 1865. The second was published on the cover of *Harper's Weekly Magazine* on March 14, 1874.

Source: The Library of Congress / Public Domain

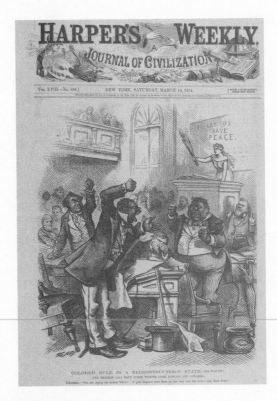

Source: The Library of Congress / Public Domain

FOUR-CORNER ANNOTATION:

POV: German-born political cartoonist, Lincoln supporter

HC: 13th Amendment, Reconstruction, Black Congressmen

PUR: Criticize Americans for not supporting the rights of Black Union soldiers after the war; criticize Black legislatures for corruption.

AUD: American readers (mostly Northerners)

SS: People in the North who were sympathetic to the cause of Black Americans began turning away from them by the end of the 1870s.

Since: Nast was such an ardent supporter of Black liberation and equality at the end of the Civil War, it's surprising to see him use racial stereotypes to demean Black legislators in the 1870s.

Document 4

Source: Heather Cox Richardson, *The Death of Reconstruction: Race, Labor and Politics in the Post–Civil War North, 1865–1901*, Harvard University Press, 2001.

In the fall of 1873, even the staunchly pro-Grant and pro-freedman *Boston Evening Transcript* ran a letter . . . arguing that "the blacks, as a people, are unfitted for the proper exercise of political duties . . . the rising generation of . . . blacks needed a period of probation and instruction; a period . . . long enough for the black to have forgotten something of his condition as a slave and learned much of the true method of gaining honorable subsistence and of performing the duties of any position to which he might aspire."

FOUR-CORNER ANNOTATION:

Claim: Northern cities had begun to turn on Black civil rights by 1873.

SS: Latent racism still existed throughout the North, which prevented some from endorsing Reconstruction policies aimed at full equality for African Americans.

DISCOURSE CYCLE (Peer-to-Peer, Then Large Group)

What arguments are these two sources making about what ended Reconstruction?

[Questions to ask if students are struggling to unpack certain key information:]

- Race problems in the South might seem of diminished importance. They also might feel more connected to political problems in DC than race problems of the deep South.

What argument is the *Boston Evening Transcript* making about Blacks in the South?

- They are arguing that Blacks had lived in slavery for so long that they weren't ready or able to participate adequately in politics and democracy.

What does the letter indicate about racism in the post–Civil War North?

- The letter shows that racism was pervasive after the Civil War, even in places like Boston, which had been the epicenter of the abolitionist movement.

Launch Inquiry Discussion	If time permits within the class period, move to the Inquiry Lesson. Otherwise, plan to teach the Inquiry Lesson in the next class.

	Inquiry Lesson
Activate Knowledge (if needed) 5–15 min	**Activate Skills and Knowledge**

	Inquiry Prompt:
	 • Who or what ultimately ended Reconstruction?
	 Review Notes:
	 • Review notes from the grappling with evidence: four-corner annotations, significance statements and preliminary thesis. Call on students to read and mark up the inquiry prompt.
	 Recall the Unpacking of the Prompt:
	 • Turn and talk, share out:
	    ○ "In your own words, what is this question asking you to do?"
	    ○ "What's the historical thinking skill embedded in the question?"

Guide Discourse 10–12 min	**Evaluate Arguments**
	Launch Discourse with a **Response to Data:** "Let's begin: Who or what ultimately ended Reconstruction?" **Discourse Cycle (whole group sprinkled with turn and talk and Everybody Writes):** Chart the arguments and evidence that is used to corroborate— prompt for whatever is missing: *Students may choose an argument that falls outside of the North and the South. For example, a student could argue that the inability of the federal government to adequately enforce the Constitution was what ultimately ended Reconstruction. They could also argue on more narrow grounds (for example, that the Panic of 1873 ended Reconstruction because it took Northern attention away from the cause and allowed Southerners to circumvent civil rights legislation).*

South killed Reconstruction	North killed Reconstruction
• Rise of hate groups like KKK systematically terrorized federal institutions set up to enforce Reconstruction policies.	• Grant administration corruption took attention and political capital away from Reconstruction.
• Southern hate groups like KKK and White League sought to actively undermine efforts at racial equality.	• Panic of 1873 caused economic problems that Northerners considered more pressing.
• Black political leaders and white supporters of Reconstruction threatened and attacked with violence.	• Racism in the North used to prevent many from fully supporting Reconstruction efforts in the South.
• Redeemers retook many Southern governments and enshrined white supremacists in the government **(prior knowledge evidence).**	• Compromise of 1877 removed federal troops **(prior knowledge evidence).**

Sophisticate Prompts:

Are the reasons for the end of Reconstruction surprising? Why or why not?

Did the official end of Reconstruction in 1877 ensure that it would ultimately fail? Why or why not?

| Revise and Stamp 3 min | **Lock in the Learning** |

Crystallize the Possible Theses/Arguments (can add more):

- (From HW reading) The Compromise of 1877 handed Republican candidate Rutherford Hayes the presidency in exchange for withdrawing the last federal troops from the South. This effectively left it up to states to enforce Reconstruction legislation and policies.

- The Panic of 1873 and economic scandals of the Grant administration shook the nation economically and diverted attention from civil rights. Support for Reconstruction in the North waned as Americans focused on solving economic and political problems and lingering racism continued to cause some Northerners to withhold support.

- The rise of the KKK and White League in the South systematically denied African Americans rights that were supposed to be guaranteed by the Constitution and Reconstruction laws. They used violence and intimidation to restore white supremacy across the South.

Stamp the Takeaways—Argumentation and Metacognition

Revise the thesis or (time permitting) write a full DBQ paragraph or essay:

Directions: Respond to the question below using specific evidence from today's class.

Who or what ultimately killed Reconstruction?

Thesis that establishes a line of reasoning—for example:

Although Reconstruction ended officially in 1877 when Hayes removed federal troops from the South, the policies of Reconstruction were already in decline. Southerners were actively subverting and ignoring policies to bring about racial equality. Northerners were turning their attention away from Reconstruction to face what they felt were more pressing political and economic problems. Ultimately the North killed Reconstruction because they won the war and it was their responsibility to ensure that the policies they had championed after the war were properly enforced. It was unrealistic to expect the South to change its ways without continued oversight and vigilance.

Topic sentences (what is each of your body paragraphs about?):

- The South helped end Reconstruction by actively trying to undermine efforts to enforce its policies and laws.

- The North also contributed to the end of Reconstruction by slowly withdrawing their support for its policies.

SAMPLE LESSON PLANS—WESTERNIZATION OR SOUTHERNIZATION? (AP WORLD HISTORY)

Most of us are familiar with the term *Westernization*. In Part 2, we introduced the arguments of several historians—Jared Diamond, J. R. McNeill, and Lydia Shaffer—who each proposed conflicting understanding for the rise of the West. Diamond based Europe's rise on geography,[1] which McNeill critiqued as overly deterministic.[2] Shaffer posited that the Western world rose to dominance by adopting technologies and sciences that came from the non-Western world—the South (Southern China).[3] She calls this spread *Southernization*, and places it in direct conflict with Westernization.

What follows are the lesson plans that World History teacher Edward Acosta used to teach a unit on Westernization versus Southernization: build knowledge, grapple with evidence, and inquiry.

Monday	Tuesday	Wednesday	Thursday	Friday
			Lesson 1 **LP Type:** Build Knowledge **Topic:** *Guns, Germs, and Steel.* **SWBAT:** Analyze Diamond's central argument in *Guns, Germs, and Steel.* • **HTS:** causation • **Resources:** Kim Marshall's summary of *Guns, Germs, and Steel* • **Key Terms:** Neolithic, domestication, immunity • **Homework:** *The Silk Roads,* "Road of Gold" chapter	**Lesson 2** **LP Type:** Build Knowledge (Guided Practice) **Topic:** Annotation Methods for Second Sources **SWBAT:** Determine author's central argument in a secondary source using margin notes and end notes. • **HTS:** "Soft Skills" • **Resources:** 1491 "Tawantinsuyu" • **Key Terms:** terrace farming, Inca, Andes, Aztec, mita, bureaucracy, Tenochtitlan
			Week 2	

Cycle Topic (Content): Interrogating the "Rise of the West"
- **Cycle Essential Question: What factors explain the rise of Western Europe in the Early Modern Era?**

Monday	Tuesday	Wednesday	Thursday	Friday
Lesson 3 **LP Type:** Build Knowledge **Topic:** Methods and Motives of European Exploration **SWBAT:** Identify the causes and impacts of 15th century European exploration of the Americas. • **HTS:** Causation, Periodization • **Resources:** Peter Frankopan, *The Silk Roads*, "The Road of Gold," 2016, pp. 204–209, 211 • **Key Terms:** Columbus, Aztecs, Cortes, Ottomans, Constantinople, spice trade, Silk Roads, demand, gunpowder • **Skill focus:** thesis • **Homework:** *A History of the World in 100 Objects*, "Double-Headed Serpent"	**Lesson 4** **LP Type:** Grapple with Evidence **Topic:** Spanish Conquest **SWBAT:** Evaluate the traditional narrative of the Spanish conquest of the Aztecs to determine the extent to which it is a valid historical interpretation. • **HTS:** causation, contextualization • **Resources:** Stanford History Education Group, Matthew Restall, "Seven Myths of the Spanish Conquest" • **Key Terms:** Cortes, Montezuma, Aztecs, smallpox • **Skill focus:** sourcing • **Homework:** McNeill, pp. 1–2	**Lesson 5** **LP Type:** Grapple with Evidence **Topic:** McNeill Article **SWBAT:** Analyze McNeill's central argument in "The World According to Jared Diamond." • **HTS:** Causation, argumentation • **Resources:** J. R. McNeill, "The World According to Jared Diamond," 2001 • **Key Terms:** geographical determinism • **Homework:** Finish McNeill and Vocab Review	**Lesson 6** **LP Type:** Inquiry **Topic:** Diamond versus McNeill **SWBAT:** Evaluate the arguments presented by Jared Diamond and J. R. McNeill concerning European conquest of the Americas. • **HTS:** Causation, argumentation • **Resources:** Kim Marshall's summary of *Guns, Germs, and Steel* and J. R. McNeill, "The World According to Jared Diamond," 2001 • **Key Terms:** Cortes, Montezuma, Aztecs, smallpox • **Skill focus:** thesis **QUIZ:** Unit 1 Vocabulary • **Homework:** Southernization article	**Lesson 7** **LP Type:** Assessment **SWBAT:** Identify evidence in support of a historian's argument and explain cause of historiographical disagreement. • **HTS:** Argumentation, Interpretation • **Resources:** Released SAQ from College Board • **Key Terms:** agriculture, sedentary, domestication • **Skill focus:** Short answer question • **Homework:** Southernization article

Build Knowledge Lesson

Build Knowledge Lesson	
Teacher: Acosta	Date:
Course: Advanced Placement World History	**Unit Title:** Interrogating "The Rise of the West"
Objective	
Skills/Content: *By the end of today's lesson, what will students know and be able to do?* SWBAT. . . • Identify the causes and impacts of European exploration during the late 15th century.	**Assessment:** *How will students demonstrate mastery of the objective?* By. . . • Creating a graphic organizer and writing a thesis in response to today's question

Prepare	**Identify the Knowledge Students Need**

Identify the Knowledge Students Need:

Key Conceptual Understandings: What key ideas do students need to take away from today's lesson?

European exploration in the late 15th century was motivated by the quest for direct access to the spice trade of South East Asia as well as the acquisition of gold and enslaved people from West Africa. The Ottoman conquest of Constantinople in 1453 was a crucial turning point that marked the end of the Byzantine Empire and prompted Western Europeans to seek a maritime route to Asia, where they could have direct access to the spice trade, rather than having to pay the Arab or Italian city-state middlemen. Importantly, European explorers adapted Asian navigational technologies from the Classical and Post-Classical eras: the compass, astrolabe, stern-post rudder, and triangular lateen sails. This technology was essential for long-distance maritime voyages.

Spanish exploration of the Americas quickly led to the decimation of the native peoples, who lacked immunity to European diseases. Those who didn't die from disease were used as forced laborers. Not long after the initial "discovery," the Spanish began to import enslaved laborers from Africa, which marked the beginning of the trans-Atlantic slave trade. Ultimately, "the rise of Europe" was made possible by the adaption of Asian technologies and the exploitation of native American and African populations.

Activate Knowledge 5–15 min	**Launch the Class**

Do Now: Cornell Notes Quiz

READING QUIZ (5 min + 90 sec trade and grade) (Focus on questions 2 and 4)

1. Which of the following had been colonized by Iberian powers BEFORE Columbus "discovered" the Americas in 1492?

   a. Greenland and Iceland

   b. Malacca and the Spice Islands

   c. **Canary Islands, Madeira, and Azores**

   d. Calicut, India

2. During the 15th century, Catholics of the Iberian Peninsula regarded which other faith as their central enemy?

   a. Protestants

   b. **Muslims**

   c. Hindus

   d. Buddhists

3. Which European power established the Trans-Atlantic slave trade?
   a. England
   b. France
   c. Spain
   d. **Portugal**

4. Which precious metal were Europeans hoping to find by exploring the coast of West Africa? **gold**

5. Which of the following did Columbus find in the Caribbean?
   a. Gold mines
   b. Cinnamon
   c. Cloves
   d. Pepper
   e. **None of the above**

6. What is the name of the Spanish conquistador who led the conquest of the Aztecs? **Cortes**

7. Which of the following does NOT include a factor that allowed the Spanish to conquer the Aztecs?
   a. The Spanish introduced diseases which the natives were not immune to.
   b. The Spanish formed alliances with rival groups.
   c. **The wealth of the Spanish, compared with the poverty of the Aztecs**
   d. The Spanish used extremely violent tactics.

- EXTRA CREDIT: What is the name of the Indigenous group that Columbus first encountered in the Caribbean? **Taíno**

Class Oral Review

- Knowledge Organizer 1.1: Navigational Technology and Aztecs

Tell a Memorable Story

Hook

Source: The Library of Congress / Public Domain

"Last week we unpacked Diamond's central argument in *Guns*, *Germs*, *and Steel*, seeking to answer why the Spanish were able to conquer the Aztec and Inca. What were some of the "immediate reasons" Diamond offers to explain this victory?"

[Call on one or two students: *horses, superior weaponry, immunity to diseases, writing systems, highly organized political system, navigational technology*]

"But why did the Europeans begin exploring in the first place? What explains the transition from the inwardly focused, isolated medieval Western Europe of the Post-Classical Era, to the global empire building Western Europe of the Early Modern Era?"

[30 sec turn and talk—What were the causes of European exploration in the 15th century?]

[Share out (*Answers should be based on* Silk Roads *reading—quest for gold, spices, enslaved people, power. . .*).

"Today, we're going to zoom in even further on this key turning point . . ."

Set the Stage:

Activate Knowledge/Activate Skill—Unpack the Source and Prompt

Call on student to read prompt: What were the causes and impacts of European exploration in the 15th century?

"Looking ahead to tomorrow, I want to preview for you that we will be diving into an Inquiry Lesson interrogating popular narratives—or versions—of the Spanish conquest of the Aztecs. How will today prepare us for next week?"

- *To build the historical context needed to understand tomorrow's documents on the conquest*

"Based on the prompt, what historical thinking skill will we be mostly using today?"

- *Causation*

Pre-Reading:

"Turn with me to the first page of your *Silk Roads* reading. You now have 5 minutes to independently complete the row of your graphic organizer on p. 2 of your packet—one cause and one impact."

Peer Groups:

Work in small groups to compare notes and identify and describe the remaining causes and impacts of European exploration.

Tell a Story

EUROPEAN EXPLORATION IN THE 15TH CENTURY—Causes and Impacts

[NOTE: Students will take Cornell notes during the lecture.]

"Frankopan opens this chapter of *The Silk Roads* by stating, "The world changed in the late 15th century." Of course, we know that 1492 marked a crucial turning point as Columbus encountered the Americas. But as you've read in Frankopan, Columbus intended to sail to India. We're going to add some important historical context to our notes on the causes and impacts of European exploration in the 15th century.

CAUSES

Spices trade–European demand and Muslim control

Europe's high demand for spices imported from Asia (pepper, cloves, cinnamon, and ginger) made the spice trade a lucrative business. Spices were a commodity (an agricultural product that could be bought or sold) for which European customers were willing to pay high prices. By the 15th century, Muslim traders had gained a significant stake in the spice trade market, which concerned Europeans. These traders worked closely with Venetians to distribute the spices to the wider European market. Although the Catholic Church attempted to disrupt this trade link by banning trade with the Muslim world, the Venetians found workarounds or ignored these mandates. Muslim influence in the region continued to increase as the Ottoman Turks began to take over territories formally controlled by the crumbling Byzantine Empire. The years 1410–1414 marked a sharp spike in the cost of imported spices. English consumers, for example, found that pepper was eight times as expensive as it used to be. This inflation prompted Europe to more seriously consider ways to establish direct trade relationships with Asia through new trade routes unknown to Muslim traders.

Source: Tom Standage's *An Edible History of Humanity* (2009).

1453: Ottoman Conquest of Constantinople

In 1453, the Muslim Ottomans conquered the last remnant of the Byzantine Empire—the capital city of Constantinople. As you see on the map, Constantinople was a strategic location for trade, connecting the East and the West, and the entry way to the Black Sea. Christian animosity toward Muslims was still very strong after centuries of Crusade battles that pitted these two faiths against each other. As such, the Ottoman conquest of Constantinople solidified the European "need" to find a maritime route to Asia—cutting out the middleman once and for all.

Reconquista

As you saw in our reading, religion also played a part in the exploration. While it would come to dominate the narrative of European expansion perhaps more than it should, the desire to win converts to Christianity was an important motivation for exploration. This sentiment was especially strong in the Iberian Peninsula—Spain and Portugal—who had been under Moorish rule for nearly 700 years (remember Al-Andalus from 9th-grade?). The Catholics of Spain had fought a centuries-long battle, the "Reconquista" to reconquer Spain from the Muslim Moors. The battle finally ended in 1492, and the Catholic monarchs, Ferdinand and Isabel, took two significant actions: (1) they commissioned Columbus's voyage and (2) they expelled all Jews and Muslims from Spain.

Asian navigational technology

European sailors adapted earlier Asian navigational technologies that allowed them to make long-distance ocean voyages. They used the magnetic compass, developed in Classical Era China, to navigate, and the astrolabe—which originated in Classical Greece but was reintroduced by Arab sailors—to determine latitude. They also revised Asian ship design. The Portuguese caravel used triangular lateen sails first introduced during the Classical Era by Asian sailors in the Indian Ocean. Another crucial Asian invention was the stern-post rudder, which more effectively steered large ships. Finally, Europeans built upon Asian knowledge of monsoon winds in the Indian Ocean to determine the "volta do mar" (return of the sea), which allowed them to navigate the Atlantic Ocean using similar strategies. What is clear is that European exploration was made possible by the adaptation of earlier Asian technology.

IMPACTS

We will spend the rest of this quarter unpacking the impacts of the rise of Europe, and specifically the conquest and colonization of the Americas. But, as you found from the reading, the growth in power and wealth of Europe went hand in hand with the decimation of the Native American population—the Taíno, the Indigenous population that inhabited the modern-day Caribbean were decimated by European arrival due to disease and violence. The destruction of the Native American population was followed by the forced migration of what would—over several centuries—amount to 20 million Africans violently taken from their homeland to endure a life of slavery in the "New World" for the benefit of Europeans.

Check for Understanding 15–20 min

Check for Understanding:

Monitor

Monitor student note-taking:

- Highlight strong notes.
- Prompt students to elaborate where notes are sparse.

Check for Understanding

Peer-to-peer:

- Team up students to review notes and the textbook pre-reading to create a concept map of the causes and impacts of European exploration in the 15th century.

What were the causes & impacts of European exploration in the 15th century?

CAUSES	IMPACTS
GOLD pp. 198-199	**IBERIAN COLONIES IN AFRICA** pp. 200-1
• Columbus's voyage was actually part of longer period of exploration by Iberian Peninsula (Spain & Portugal) to <u>access gold markets of W.Africa</u> (198) • Wealth of region was "legendary," and encapsulated by Mansa Musa of Mali (199)	• Expeditions led to discovery of Canary Islands, Madeira and Azores → climate & rich soil → sugar cane cultivation → exported (200) • Portuguese established colonies along West coast of Africa to establish control over important sea lanes (201) • Portuguese established a royal monopoly on trade to/with Africa (201)

Additional Causes/Motivations: Impacts:

SLAVES pp. 202-3	COERCED LABOR pp. 202, 207, 211
• Demand for manpower to work on farms and plantations in Portugal (202) • Portuguese kept sailing further southward along coast of Africa in search of "prey," and as they continued further south, they found that settlements were less well defended (203)	• Beginning of Trans-Atlantic slave trade in 1400s: Slave raids tore apart families and communities in West Africa (202-3) • Forced labor of Taino and other Native Americans (207)
SPICES pp. 204-5	DISCOVERY OF PRECIOUS METALS p. 206
• Columbus reported back to the Spanish king and queen that he had found cinnamon, rhubarb and aloe in the Caribbean Islands -- which he was convinced were off the coast of India (204-5)	• On his third voyage, Columbus and his crew encountered a large quantity of pearls in Venezuela (206) • While no substantial supply of gold was discovered in the Caribbean where Columbus first landed (204), shortly after, the Spanish discovered gold and silver in Central and South America (206)
RELIGION p. 201, 211	CONQUEST & DECIMATION OF NATIVES p. 207
• Iberian Peninsula (Spain & Portugal) harbored intense animosity toward Islam and Muslim merchants, and resented their control over profitable trade routes and goods (201) • Purpose of colonization, according to some religious leaders "was to glorify the Catholic faith and save souls" not to make money (211)	• Taino pop. fell from 500,000 – 2,000 in a few decades due brutal treatment by the Spanish and the introduction of European diseases (207) • Cortes and the conquistadores conquered the Aztecs using violence and alliances (207-8)

Class oral review:

• Ask key questions to check for their understanding of the lecture.
• Chart for reference.

Exit Ticket:

• Explain the historical context that gave rise to the age of European exploration and eventually conquest in the 15th century.
• Remind them of thesis statement structures:
  ○ Although/While (general statement about counterargument)
  ○ nevertheless/ultimately (your thesis/argument)
  ○ because (summary of your key evidence 1, 2, 3, etc.)

Potential Response:

While the desire to spread Christianity around the world motivated some Europeans to take part in exploration in the 15th century, ultimately this wave of exploration was driven by the quest for direct access to the spice trade of South East Asia because this would allow Europeans to take part in the highly lucrative trade.

Revise:

If time, display an exemplar student response and have students analyze it. Then, provide students 2 to 4 more minutes to revise their work.

Grapple with Evidence and Inquiry Lessons

If time doesn't permit, split the lesson over two class periods.

GRAPPLE WITH EVIDENCE	
Objectives	• Evaluate Diamond's central claim that history has been largely determined by geography.
Texts	• Kim Marshall's summary of *Guns, Germs, and Steel* by Jared Diamond (1997) • J. R. McNeill, "The World According to Jared Diamond" (2001)
Questions	1. **Round 1 Question:** According to Jared Diamond, how did Eurasian geography provide an advantage to the Spanish in their conquest of the Aztec and Inca Empires? 2. **Round 2 Question:** How does McNeill undermine Diamond's argument in *Guns, Germs, and Steel*? What are the main elements of his counterargument? 3. **Round 3 Question:** To what extent is history determined by geography? Whose argument do you find more compelling—Diamond or McNeill?
Pre-Work	• Summer assignment—Marshall's summary of *Guns, Germs, and Steel* • Small Group Seminar—analyzed Diamond's argument • McNeill close read
Set Up	On their desks, students should have: • 1.1 graphic organizer—*Guns, Germs, and Steel* • 1.5 graphic organizer—McNeill critique (last night's PW) • Both articles—Diamond and McNeill

Activate Knowledge 10–15 min	**Do Now** (5 MIN WORK TIME + 5 MIN REVIEW TO CLARIFY MISUNDERSTANDINGS) **Ask:** According to Diamond, what factors allowed European countries (8% of the world) to conquer and colonize 84% of the world by the end of the 1600s?

IMMEDIATE	LONG-TERM
1. **Superior weaponry** (rifles and cannons vs. swords)	1. **GEOGRAPHIC LUCK** – Europe was part of Eurasia, which had MANY usable domesticated animals (horse, pig, cow, sheep, goat) while the Americas had only one large animal that humans could tame and put to work (alpaca/llama).
2. **Horses** (mounted cavalry = terrifying and effective weapon → military advantage, despite being outnumbered)	
3. **Ships and navigation methods**	2. **Agriculture → civilization**
4. **Writing system** that allowed for rapid communication	3. **Agriculture (and other technology) <u>spread</u> from its origin in Fertile Crescent <u>along East–West axis</u> for two reasons:**
5. **Highly centralized political organization** that allowed governments to fund expeditions	• These plants and animals could thrive best in fairly narrow E-W latitude band.
6. **Infectious diseases** which decimated the native populations, weakening their resistance capacity	• Fertile Crescent is part of Eurasia, oriented E-W, different than Americas, Africa.
<u>NOT</u>: Europeans were more intelligent, cold winters in Europe spurred ingenuity and invention, others were more peace-loving and Europeans were violent, God favored Christian Europe	4. **Domesticated animals led to immunity → ability to live near animals and infected people without getting sick**

Anticipated Misunderstandings:

• Students miss Diamond's claim that geography has largely determined the success of the Eurasian landmass.

• Students don't differentiate between "immediate reasons" for Spanish conquest of Aztec and Inca and Diamond's larger geographic determinist argument about "luck" of Middle East/Eurasian landmass.

	ACTIVATE KNOWLEDGE—CLASS ORAL REVIEW (5 MIN) 1. The Americas are a part of which hemisphere? *Western* 2. Chinese military innovation that was transferred westward to Europe by way of the Arabs and Mongols during the Post-Classical Era? *Gunpowder* 3. Who conquered the Inca? *Pizarro* 4. Aztecs? *Hernan Cortes* 5. The native population of the Caribbean who were decimated by violence and disease shortly after the arrival of Europeans? *Taíno* 6. A technological innovation developed in Asia that Europeans adapted, which allowed them to make long-distance oceanic voyages in the Early Modern Era? *compass, astrolabe, stern-post rudder, triangular sails, knowledge of monsoon winds* 7. Native American populations were devastated by the introduction of Europeans and their livestock because they lacked immunity to these foreign diseases.
Set the Stage 7 min recommended	Every day in APWH, we strive to think like historians, as outlined by our historical thinking skills. Today, we will be **evaluating** two oppositional perspectives on the development of civilizations. You must decide which argument is most persuasive and historically defensible. **Orient participants in the materials:** You will need: • 1.2 graphic organizer—*Guns, Germs, and Steel* • 1.6 graphic organizer – McNeill critique (last night's PW) • Both articles—Diamond and McNeill **Discourse Cycle:** In small groups or partners (depending on class size/arrangement), students will discuss seminar Questions 1 and 2. Teacher will circulate to determine trend, then launch whole-group seminar.

Discourse, Round 1		
Discourse Round 1 14 min recommended	**Round 1 Question:** According to Jared Diamond, how did Eurasian geography provide an advantage to the Spanish in their conquest of the Aztec and Inca Empires?	
	Core Idea and Key Evidence	**Prompts**
	Core Idea 1—<u>E-W axis orientation allowed for spread of agriculture from Fertile Crescent to both edges of Eurasia.</u>	
	Key Evidence: Fertile Crescent was "lucky" as it had 5 out of the 14 land mammals that are good for domestication (cows, sheep, goats, pigs, horses) and a plethora of plants from wild cereals, grains, and legumes to fruits and nuts.	Jared Diamond bases his argument in geography. What aspects of Eurasia's geography does he argue provided an advantage?
	Agriculture spread along the East-West axis via "comfort zone"/latitude range → Western Europe benefited from agricultural advancements Fertile Crescent.	What were the advantages of the "E-W axis"?
	E-W axis <u>facilitated competition</u> between Eurasian peoples → Competition and war further accelerated <u>development of tech</u>—from agriculture, weapons, writing → the development of advanced civilization proceeded quickly in Eurasia	
	<u>Africa & Americas – oriented along N-S axis</u>, → prevented spread of agriculture and other tech → Advancements couldn't be shared and built upon by other regions	
	IMPACT ON SPANISH CONQUEST: <u>Europeans benefited from technologies developed as far away as China</u>—such as gunpowder for superior weaponry, paper for <u>written communication</u>, wheel for transportation, and the <u>navigational tools</u>	

like the compass, astrolabe, and rudder, which were essential for crossing the Atlantic—that gave them an advantage over the Aztecs, who, according to Diamond, developed more isolation from other civilizations due to the N-S orientation of the American continent.

E-W axis also gave the Spanish the horses they would use to fight Aztec and Inca soldiers on foot.

Which continents does Diamond argue had N-S orientation? What was the impact?

How did the E-W orientation provide the Spanish with an advantage over the Aztecs?

Core Idea 2—Proximity to domesticated animals led to immunity to infectious diseases

Key Evidence:

Living close to domesticated animals → variety of highly fatal diseases, such as measles and smallpox from cattle or influenza from pigs and ducks → diseases spread quickly → long term, those who survived developed antibodies or inherited immunity → protect them against future infection from that disease.

Those on other continents—especially the Americas—who did not have contact with these domesticated animals, did not build immunity. This led to fatal consequences when they encountered Eurasians and their domesticated animals carrying these diseases.

IMPACT ON SPANISH CONQUEST:

When the Spanish arrived in the Caribbean in 1492, the germs/diseases they carried would soon decimate the native population.

→ Weaken resistance

→ Easy victory for Spanish

Diamond highlights the role of the Neolithic Revolution—the beginnings of agriculture—as essential to the development of all civilizations. What "advantages" does he argue Eurasia, or more specifically, the Fertile Crescent, had?

We've discussed plants—how about animals?

What were the immediate impacts of living close to domesticated animals?

How about the long-term impacts?

How did centuries of living in proximity to domesticated animals provide Europeans with an advantage in the Americas?

Stamp

Stamp

Must haves:

- E-W axis facilitated transfer of technology across Eurasia, which facilitated the rapid development of advanced civilizations.

- Eurasian peoples' proximity to domesticated animals over centuries provided them with immunity to animal-related diseases, an immunity that those on other continents did not have, and the consequences of which would prove fatal.

Discourse, Round 2		
Discourse Round 2 14 min recommended	**Round 2 Question:** How does McNeill undermine Diamond's argument in *Guns, Germs, and Steel*? What are the main elements of his counterargument?	
	Core Idea and Key Evidence	**Questions to Prompt if Students Are Struggling**
	Core Idea 1—<u>Eurasia's</u> dominance can't explain <u>Europe's</u> dominance. **<u>Key Evidence [P9 and P12]:</u>** Eurasia accounted for 80% of humankind over past 3,000 years → formidability would of course be located where the vast majority of world's population is. Greater pop → greater interaction → more intense intersocietal competition → immunity That Diamond even thought this was an interesting question (Why Eurasia was dominant) is not so "perplexing." McNeill argues that Diamond has pushed his argument too far by trying to answer the "Why Europe?" question through geography. Diamond's geography argument explains Eurasia's dominance, but assumes that would also explain Western Europe's dominance BUT Western Europe is only a small portion of Eurasia.	Diamond spends a lot of energy developing his argument for why Eurasia became so dominant. What issue does McNeill see with this? Historians are interested in the "Why Europe?" question—with this in mind, what is the flaw within Diamond's argument for European dominance?
	Core Idea 2—Europe's geography (which led to <u>political fragmentation</u>) alone cannot explain its dominance. **<u>Key Evidence [P10–P11]:</u>** Europe's advantage was based in its geography is NOT a new idea. But more than this, it's not a logical conclusion.	What aspect of Europe's topography/geography does Diamond highlight as a strength? What evidence does McNeill use to demonstrate the flaw within Diamond's claim? When has political fragmentation NOT been an advantage?

It is logically impossible to explain a temporary phenomenon (i.e., dominance of Europe in certain centuries) by reference to permanent conditions (geography).

Political fragmentation can be a weakness

- EV: division of Africa and India → European control

- EV: Medieval Europe was divided and not powerful

To explain "Why Europe?," part of answer must be temporary.

Core Idea 3—The successful spread of useful species (livestock and crops) was NOT due to the E-W latitude "comfort zone," but instead was usually a conscious, human act—trade links and migration usually spread these species.

Key Evidence [P15–16]:

Eurasia's E-W axis would NOT have helped the spread of domesticated animals:

- EV: Eurasia's extreme variety of climactic conditions from high mountains and deserts to tropical forests posed a challenge for spread of most animals, and likely plants.

Most useful species were spread by conscious human acts:

- EV: Coffee, native to Ethiopia → Brazil

- EV: Cattle, native to SW Asia → S. Africa and Sweden (became essential in Europe, inconsequential in China)

To describe the underlying issue within Diamond's argument, McNeill compares permanent versus temporary things. What is the issue here?

What issue does McNeill see in the E-W axis theory that Diamond proposes?

Let's zoom in to P16. How are "useful species" spread according to McNeill? What evidence does he use to support his argument?

Overall, what is the CAUSE of a society's success or failure, according to Diamond? (geography)

What issue does McNeill have with this? Let's zoom in to the end of P18. What other factors have influenced the development of societies?

In P20, what does McNeill argue is the danger of basing our understanding of the world—and likelihood that any region will be powerful—on geography?

	Core Idea 4—Contrary to Diamond's central claim, the fate of human societies is not wholly determined by geography and developments that took place in 8000 BCE. It is important to underscore that humans shape their environment. People DO help shape their environment—a fact that Diamond acknowledges when (1) he claims the Middle East "committed ecological suicide" and (2) Americas and Australia hunted their large land mammals to extinction.	
	Round 3 Question: To what extent is history determined by geography? Whose argument do you find more compelling—Diamond or McNeill?	
	Arguments and evidence will vary, but teacher should direct students to key points in both articles: **Diamond:** • Middle East had strikingly large number of plants and animals that could be domesticated, which led to this civilization emerging first, allowing agriculture to spread E-W. • Eurasia's domestication of animals gave them immunity to infectious diseases, but also made them a deadly force when confronted with new populations not exposed to such animals. **McNeill:** • Being the vast majority of the world's population, it was very likely that Eurasia would give birth to its strongest civilizations (P9). • Diamond may effectively make the case for Eurasia, but his argument does not effectively answer "Why Europe?".	What are Diamond's strongest points that would be difficult to undermine? What are McNeill's strongest counterclaims?

Final Writing Task	**Final Writing Task:**
	• To what extent is history determined by geography?
	• Remind them of thesis statement structures:
	○ Although/While (general statement about counterargument)
	○ nevertheless/ultimately (your thesis/argument)
	○ because (summary of your key evidence 1, 2, 3, etc.)
	Potential Exemplar Thesis:
	<u>While</u> history has been somewhat determined by geography, as seen in the case of the Spanish conquest of the Aztec and Inca, which was largely due to the impact of Eurasian diseases on the native population, <u>ultimately</u> human acts like trade and migration played a more crucial role in shaping the development of societies <u>because</u> they result in the transfer of key technologies that aid the rise of states.

Conclusion

"Our histories cling to us. We are shaped by where we come from."
—Chimamanda Ngozi Adichie

"History, skillfully applied and deeply understood, can save the world."
—Patricia Limerick

In his 1935 book, *Black Reconstruction*, W.E.B. Du Bois sought to challenge the damaging and incomplete, but common, narrative about the failings of Reconstruction in the South in the years following the US Civil War. At the time of Du Bois's writing, historians and textbooks throughout the country, like those from the Dunning School, propagated the idea that Reconstruction failed due to the aggressive overreach of carpetbagger Northerners, the ineptitude and corruption of Black office holders in the South, and the general immaturity and irresponsible nature of a Black society ill-prepared for the civil rights afforded by the efforts of Reconstruction. In a chapter titled "The Propaganda of History," from his book, Du Bois questioned the ways in which the story of Reconstruction was being studied and taught at the time.

Excerpt from Black Reconstruction

Source: W.E.B. Du Bois, *Black Reconstruction*, 1935.

If history is going to be scientific, if the record of human action is going to be set down with the accuracy and faithfulness of detail which will allow its use as a measuring rod and guidepost for the future of nations, there must be set some standards of ethics in research and interpretation.

If, on the other hand, we are going to use history for our pleasure and amusement, for inflating our national ego, and giving us a false but pleasurable sense of accomplishment, then we must give up the idea of history as a science or as an art using the results of science, and admit frankly that we are using a version of historic fact in order to influence and educate the new generation along the way we wish.

It is propaganda like this that has led men in the past to insist that history is "lies agreed upon"; and to point out the danger in such misinformation. It is indeed extremely doubtful if any permanent benefit comes to the world through such action.[1]

The story of Reconstruction is just one example of how a single, dominant narrative can define a moment in time and how we are taught to think about it. But history, as a discipline, gives us tools to think differently and arrive at our own conclusions. In Part 6, we saw how Amir's students use all the moves we've described in *Make History* to unravel and rebuild the story. Starting from a shared narrative of events, they delve into multiple sources. Some will speak to each other to corroborate evidence, while others may seemingly contradict all or part of an account. Students hear from a multitude of voices, especially those that may have been traditionally silenced and forgotten; this helps them do the disciplinary work with integrity. And discourse is the arena to answer provocative inquiry questions to form, challenge, and strengthen unique arguments.

It is through the collaborative work of rigorous sensemaking that students become historians.

History is messy. It is complicated and full of people and societies capable of great achievements and brutal atrocities. It is by embracing that messiness, and guiding our students to do the same, that we come to understand our world and what it means to be human. Conversely, if we never work to hone our students' disciplinary thinking and skills, or if we aim to limit the voices and perspectives from the past in order to serve our own biases, we are no longer engaged in the discipline of history. History then becomes propaganda. Du Bois closed this chapter of *Black Reconstruction* with a powerful call to his readers. "Nations reel and stagger on their way; they make hideous mistakes; they commit frightful wrongs; they do great and beautiful things. And shall we not best guide humanity by telling the truth about all this, so far as the truth is ascertainable?"[2]

The past has much to teach us, and it shapes us today. I (Art) have personally felt the power of what a knowledge of the past can do; it has literally shaped my understanding of the people I love the most. I was not able to finish my father's memoir with him before he became too sick to continue. Yet I'm thankful for every single moment I was able to share with him. Those moments built a deeper understanding of my own identity and purpose, and of what it will take to bring real social justice to our country for the first time.

We are so grateful to share the work of teaching history with teachers who have chosen to embrace the messiness of history in this way, at a time when political and societal pressures do not always make it easy to do so. It is our hope that this book will provide tools and resources to help history educators in the important work of supporting our students as sensemakers who do more than learn stories of the past. With our help, our students can become well informed, empathetic disciplinary thinkers who are able to make history in their own right.

Notes

INTRODUCTION

1. Zaretta Hammond, *Culturally Responsive Teaching and the Brain: Promoting Authentic Engagement and Rigor among Culturally and Linguistically Diverse Students* (Corwin, 2015).

PART 1

1. Jonathan Bassett and Gary Shiffman, *From Story to Judgment: The Four Question Method for Teaching and Learning Social Studies* (John Catt, 2021).
2. Sam Wineburg, *Historical Thinking and Other Unnatural Acts: Charting the Future of Teaching the Past* (Temple University Press, 2001).
3. Bassett and Shiffman, *From Story to Judgment*.
4. "Great Society," Stanford History Education Group, Teacher Materials, Student Materials, Original Documents. https://sheg.stanford.edu/history-lessons/great-society.
5. Sam Wineburg and Daisy Martin. "Tampering with History: Adapting Primary Sources for Struggling Readers." *Social Education*, no. 73: 212-216.
6. "Historical Thinking Skills," AP United States History, AP Central (January 2021). https://apcentral.collegeboard.org/pdf/ap-us-history-course-overview.pdf?course=ap-united-states-history.
7. Wineburg, "Historical Thinking and Other Unnatural Acts". *The Phi Delta Kappan*, vol 80: 488–499. https://www.jstor.org/stable/20439490.
8. Sam Wineburg, "Unnatural and Essential: The Nature of Historical Thinking," *Teaching History* no. 129: 6–11. https://www.jstor.org/stable/43259304.
9. Sam Wineburg, "Unnatural and Essential."

10. Sam Wineburg, "Unnatural and Essential."

11. E. D. Hirsch's work on core knowledge dates to as far back as his 1988 text *Cultural Literacy: What Every American Needs to Know* and as recently as 2012, when he penned the article "How Schools Fail Democracy" for *The Chronicle of Higher Education.*

12. Diane F. Halpern, *Thought & Knowledge: An Introduction to Critical Thinking* (Psychology Press, 2013); Robert H. Ennis, *Critical Thinking* (Pearson, 1995).

13. See Daniel T. Willingham, *Why Don't Students Like School? A Cognitive Scientist Answers Questions About How the Mind Works and What It Means for the Classroom* (Jossey-Bass, 2010). As one additional example, in the earliest pages of *A Portrait of the Artist as Young Man*, Joyce shows adults singing "oh the wild rose blossoms" with a child, and then writes "oh the gween wothe botheth." English students may not immediately realize that what Joyce is doing is writing what it sounds like when the child sings the same song, but the tools they need to solve the puzzle are on the page, and the ideal teaching move is to try to get them to solve it themselves. *Animal Farm*, however, is easier to read but assumes a good deal of knowledge about 20th-century geopolitics. Literacy specialists Kylene Beers and Bob Probst encourage students to consider the question "What did the author think I already knew?" as a way to defang the confrontation with their own gaps in background knowledge. See Beers, Kylene, and Robert E. Probst, *Reading Nonfiction: Notice & Note Stances, Signposts, and Strategies* (Heinemann, 2016).

PART 2

1. Jared Diamond, *Gun, Germs and Steel: The Fate of Human Societies* (W. W. Norton, 1999).

2. J. R. McNeill, "The World According to Jared Diamond," *The History Teacher* 34, no. 2: 165–174. doi: https://doi.org/10.2307/3054276.

3. Lynda Shaffer, "Southernization," *Journal of World History* 5, no. 1: 1–21. http://www.jstor.org/stable/20078579.

4. Youki Terada, "Why Students Forget—and What You Can Do About It." *Edutopia* (September 20, 2017). https://www.edutopia.org/article/why-students-forget-and-what-you-can-do-about-it?utm_source=twitter&utm_medium=socialflow.

5. Pooja Agarwal, Henry Roediger, Mark McDaniel, and Kathleen McDermott, *How to Use Retrieval Practice to Improve Learning* (Washington University in St. Louis, 2020).

6. Pooja K. Agarwal and Patrice M. Bain, *Powerful Teaching: Unleash the Science of Learning* (Jossey-Bass, 2019). Visit retrievalpractice.org for free downloadable resources on how to integrate retrieval practice protocols in the classroom.

7. Zaretta Hammond, *Culturally Responsive Teaching and the Brain: Promoting Authentic Engagement and Rigor among Culturally and Linguistically Diverse Students* (Corwin, 2015), 74.

8. Agarwal and Bain, *Powerful Teaching*.

9. Jeffrey D. Karpicke, "A Powerful Way to Improve Learning and Memory," *Psychological Science Agenda* (June 2016). https://www.apa.org/science/about/psa/2016/06/learning-memory.

10. Daniel Willingham, *Why Don't Students Like School? A Cognitive Scientist Answers Questions About How the Mind Works and What It Means for Your Classroom* (Jossey-Bass, 2021).

11. Deborah Appleman, Michael Smith, and Jeff Wilhelm. *Uncommon Core: Where the Authors of the Standards Go Wrong about Instruction—And How You Can Get It Right*, (Corwin, 2014), 47.

12. Jonathan Gottschall, *The Storytelling Animal: How Stories Make Us Human* (Mariner Books, 2013).

13. Susana Martinez-Conde, Robert G. Alexander, Deborah Blum, Noah Britton, Barbara K. Lipska, Gregory J. Quirk, Jamy Ian Swiss, Roel M. Willems, and Stephen L. Macknik, "The Storytelling Brain: How Neuroscience Stories Help Bridge the Gap Between Research and Society," *The Journal of Neuroscience* 39, no. 42: 8285–8290. doi: 10.1523/JNEUROSCI.1180–19.2019.

14. Giovanni Rodriguez, "This Is Your Brain on Storytelling: The Chemistry of Modern Communication," *Forbes* (July 21, 2017). https://www.forbes.com/sites/giovannirodriguez/2017/07/21/this-is-your-brain-on-storytelling-the-chemistry-of-modern-communication/?sh=3e346e2ec865.

15. Hammond, *Culturally Responsive Teaching and the Brain*.

16. Jonathan Bassett and Gary Shiffman, *From Story to Judgment: The Four Question Method for Teaching and Learning Social Studies* (John Catt, 2021).

17. Bassett and Shiffman, *From Story to Judgment*.

PART 3

1. "Stonewall Riots," Stanford History Education Group, Teacher Materials, Student Materials, Original Documents. https://sheg.stanford.edu/history-lessons/stonewall-riots?check_logged_in=1.

2. Sylvia Rivera, speech to the Latino Gay Men of New York, June 2001. Reprinted in *Centro Journal* (Spring 2007).

3. Alexandra Osika, Stephanie MacMahon, Jason M. Lodge, and Annemaree Caroll, "Learning Challenge and Difficulty," *Times Higher Education* (March 31, 2002). https://www.timeshighereducation.com/campus/learning-challenge-and-difficulty-calm-seas-do-not-make-skilful-sailors.

4. L. S. Vygotsky, *Mind in Society: The Development of Higher Psychological Processes* (Harvard University Press, 1980).

5. Jonathan Bassett and Gary Shiffman, *From Story to Judgment: The Four Question Method for Teaching and Learning Social Studies* (John Catt, 2021).

6. Zaretta Hammond, "Preparing to Be a Culturally Responsive Practitioner," *Culturally Responsive Teaching and the Brain* (Corwin, 2015), 52–69.

PART 4

1. Will Durant, *The Story of Philosophy: The Lives and Opinions of the World's Greatest Philosophers* (Pocket Books, 1991).

2. Sarah Michaels and Catherine O'Connor. "Supporting teachers in taking up productive talk moves: The long road to professional learning at scale." *International Journal of Education Research* no. 97: 166–175. https://doi.org/10.1016/j.ijer.2017.11.003 and "Conceptualizing Talk Moves at Tools: Professional Development Approaches for Academically Productive Discussions." In L.B.Resnick, C.Asterhan and S.N. Clarke (Eds.), *Socializing Intelligence through Talk and Dialogue*, 333–347. https://doi.org/10.3102/978-0-935302-43-1_27.

3. David E. Leary, "A Moralist in an Age of Scientific Analysis and Skepticism: Habit in the Life and Work of William James," *A History of Habit: From Aristotle to Bourdieu*, edited by Tom Sparrow and Adam Hutchinson (Lexington Books, 2013), 177–208.

4. "Public Housing," Stanford History Education Group, Teacher Materials, Student Materials, Original Documents, PowerPoint. https://sheg.stanford.edu/history-lessons/public-housing.

5. Doug Lemov, "Three Types of Writing in the Classroom," *Doug Lemov's Field Notes*. Teach Like a Champion (November 13, 2017). https://teachlikeachampion.com/blog/three-types-writing-classroom/.

6. Joan Didion, *Where I Was From* (Knopf Doubleday Publishing, 2004).

7. Elham Kazemi and Deborah Stipek. "Promoting Conceptual Thinking in Four Upper-Elementary Mathematics Classrooms." *The Elementary School Journal*, no. 102:59–80. https://www.jstor.org/stable/1002169. Kazemi and Stipek refer to moves like these as "high conceptual press" for their ability to ground discourse in the essential ideas.

8. "Homestead Strike," Stanford History Education Group, Teacher Materials, Student Materials, Original Documents, PowerPoint. https://sheg.stanford.edu/history-lessons/homestead-strike.

PART 5

1. Vignette adapted from Claudia's Sutherland, "Stono Rebellion (1739)," *Black Past* 18 (September 2018). https://www.blackpast.org/african-american-history/stono-rebellion-1739/ and Peter H. Wood, *Black Majority: Negroes in Colonial South Carolina from 1670s through the Stono Rebellion.* (London: W.W. Norton and Co, 1974). http://www.pbs.org/wgbh/aia/part1/1p284.html.

2. "Slavery, Anti-Slavery, and the Atlantic Exchange," *US History (American Yawp)*, Lumen Learning. https://courses.lumenlearning.com/suny-ushistory1ay/chapter/slavery-anti-slavery-and-atlantic-exchange/.

3. Eric Foner, "Chapter 4: Slavery, Freedom, and the Struggle for Empire to 1763," *Give Me Liberty: An American History* (W. W. Norton, 2020).

4. Cindi May, "A Learning Secret: Don't Take Notes with a Laptop," *Scientific American* (June 3, 2014). https://www.scientificamerican.com/article/a-learning-secret-don-t-take-notes-with-a-laptop/.

5. Doug Lemov, "Three Types of Writing in the Classroom," *Doug Lemov's Field Notes*, 13 (November 2017). https://teachlikeachampion.com/blog/three-types-writing-classroom/.

6. Paul Bambrick-Santoyo, *Driven by Data* (Chapter 1) (Wiley, 2019).

PART 6

1. Jared Diamond, *Gun, Germs and Steel: The Fate of Human Societies* (W. W. Norton, 1999).

2. J. R. McNeill, "The World According to Jared Diamond," *The History Teacher* 34, no. 2 (2001): 165–174. doi: https://doi.org/10.2307/3054276.

3. Lynda Shaffer, "Southernization," *Journal of World History* 5, no. 1 (1994): 1–21. *Jstor*, http://www.jstor.org/stable/20078579.

CONCLUSION

1. W.E.B. Du Bois, *Black Reconstruction in America* (Free Press, 1999).
2. Du Bois, *Black Reconstruction in America*.

Index

Bias
    handling, 148–149
    unpacking, 100
Black Codes, 168
Black Reconstruction (Du Bois), 205–206
Blake, Rachel, 27, 56–58, 60–61, 67–68,
    72–73, 75, 78–79, 82–89
Bolívar, Simón, 18–19, 34, 36–37, 50, 58
Boston Tea Party, emergence, 86
Bottom-up historical perspectives,
    consideration, 35
Brain, activation, 60
Breakstone, Joel, 39
Bridges, building, 83
Bridge units, language, 83
Brinkerhoff, Tom, 128–130
Britannica source, 35
Build Knowledge Lesson one-pager, 90–91

C

Califano, Jr., Joseph A., 2, 24
Campos, Jah'Nique, 18–23, 28–29, 32–36,
    38–40, 46–50, 99
Cato's Conspiracy (Cato's Rebellion). *See*
    Stono Rebellion
Chavez, Cesar, 5
Cheat sheets, appearance, 71
Choices Program (Brown University), 27
Civil Rights Act, 2, 105, 177
Civil Rights Bill, passage, 1
Civil Rights movement
    struggle, 98
    tactics, 109
Civil War, 87, 121, 205
    aftermath, 168
    cause, 129
    class discussion, sample, 122–123
Claim, revision, 151
Class
    launch, 56–57, 172, 189–190
    oral review, 65–67, 115, 175, 195, 198
    preparation, 49–50

prompts
    crafting, 28–31
    quality, 23
Class discussion, 108
    Civil War sample, 122–123
    Great Society program sample, 2–4
    Latin American revolutions, 18–19
    Newark housing lesson, 133–134, 138
    problematizing, sample, 146–147
    prompts, breakdown/contextualization,
        102–104
    sample, 130–131
    Southernization, Westernization (contrast), 89
    Stonewall Uprising, causes, 94–96
    Stono's Rebellion, sample, 154–155
    women's liberation, 157
Class oral review
    activities, power, 66
    content, 65
    leveraging, 65–67
    skill, 67
Classroom
    culture, foundation, 66
    layout, 110–111
Coaching, in-the-minute, 113
Coercive Act, 86
Cognitive work, 140
    encouragement, writing (impact), 158
Colby, Abram, 177, 180, 181
Cold War era, 94, 105
Collaborative learning activities, 236
Collaborative sensemaking, 143
College Board DBQ tasks, 27
College Board, The (historical thinking
    skills), 38–39
Columbus, Christopher, 55–57, 89
Competency, development, 103
Comprehension
    gap, identification, 108
    monitoring, 86
Comprehensive response, writing, 49
Compromise of 1877, 122, 168, 185